ENGAGING College STUDENTS

A FUN AND EDGY GUIDE FOR PROFESSORS

Mike Kowis, Esq.

Library of Congress Control Number: 2016914138
ISBN-13: 978-0-9979946-2-9 (hardcover)
ISBN-13: 978-0-9979946-1-2 (paperback)
ISBN-13: 978-0-9979946-0-5 (eBook/MOBI format)
ISBN-13: 978-0-9979946-3-6 (eBook/EPUB format)

Lecture PRO Publishing
Conroe, TX

Table of Contents

Preface

Inspiration for this book came from the many talented and caring people I was lucky enough to call my teachers. During my impressionable teenage years, my favorite teacher was Mr. Floyd W. Scott. Unlike most teachers at Dayton High School (Dayton, Texas), Mr. Scott made a huge impression because he was constantly making an effort to grab his students' attention and make us laugh, even if that meant making a fool of himself. He was known to occasionally wear crazy hats or costumes related to the literature we were studying. It was not uncommon to hear Mr. Scott belch loudly in class and unapologetically proclaim, "that wasn't bad manners, just good beer!" He also told funny jokes, some of which included mild curse words or sexual innuendo (but never in a derogatory manner toward a particular student). For example, he once told my twelfth-grade English class a risqué joke that was first made famous by George Bernard Shaw:

A guy asks a woman, "Would you sleep with me for a million dollars?" She replies, "Yes, of course. A million dollars would change my whole life!" So he asks, "Okay, would you sleep with me for one dollar?" She gasps. "No way. What kind of woman do you think I am?" He responds, "Madam, we have already established what you are. We are merely haggling over the price."

Jokes like this made Mr. Scott something of a legend among students at Dayton High School because no other teacher in our small East Texas town would dare to utter a swear word or repeat adult jokes in front of high school students. His students actually looked forward to class because he made an honest effort to make class entertaining and enjoyable. To say the least, Mr. Scott was well-loved and respected by all of his students.

In college, my most inspiring professor was Dr. Timothy W. Clipson. In addition to being a remarkable communications professor in the business school at Stephen F. Austin State

University (Nacogdoches, Texas), he was also a motivational speaker on the weekends. Like any teacher worth his salt, Dr. Clipson had a way of motivating his students to do their very best, both in class and in their personal lives. I recall feeling excited and uplifted every time I walked out of his classroom— almost as if I had just attended Sunday church! To this day, Dr. Clipson remains a valued mentor and friend. I often thank him for his powerful and motivational teaching style, which continues to influence my work and personal life.

My most influential law professor was Mr. James M. Douglas, Esq. As a first-year law student ("1L"), I was intimidated by all of my law professors. So you can imagine how terrifying it was for me to learn that Professor Douglas was also the dean of the Thurgood Marshall School of Law (Houston, Texas). It also didn't help that he was a master at applying the Socratic teaching method in his class, which is often used to train 1Ls to carefully read the assigned cases and to use critical thinking skills (a.k.a. to "think like a lawyer").

There were also other excellent teachers who contributed to my development as a student and a person. For example, Mrs. Judy Webb was my eighth-grade English teacher at Woodrow Wilson Junior High (Dayton, Texas) and sponsor of my UIL Ready Writing team. She instilled great confidence in my ability to write and communicate creatively by encouraging me to freely express myself through writing. Another big influence was Dr. Elizabeth Brice, who taught my business law class at Stephen F. Austin State University in the spring of 1990. Her great passion for teaching and remarkable use of vivid and colorful analogies (some of which I still remember to this day) inspired me to want to learn more about the law and motivated me to read as much as possible. It's no small task to convince college students to read their assigned textbooks, but somehow Dr. Brice was able to light a fire in me to do so. Mr. L. Darnell Weeden, Esq., was one of my favorite law professors at Thurgood Marshall School of Law. He served as a mentor for my very first teaching job (his teaching assistant). His support and guidance eased my introduction to the world of teaching.

To all the folks mentioned above and everyone else who helped shape me into the college instructor I am today, I thank you with all of my heart.

Introduction: A Lifetime in the Classroom

Mr. Kowis is a phenomenal instructor who uses his sense of humor to relay Business Law in a way that is fun and educational at the same time. I have NEVER met an instructor who is as powerful as he is and cares whether his students are actually learning or not. He ensures that you get the material and gives EVERYONE the opportunity to ask questions and participate in the classroom learning experience. This is a class that you will enjoy. He takes a three-hour long evening course and turns it into an amazing two-part learning experience that you'll never forget! He is by far the best instructor I've learned from.

—Anonymous student evaluation from Fall 2013

Believe it or not, I have spent most of my lifetime in one classroom or another. After graduating from high school in 1988, I pursued higher education for the next eight years at Stephen F. Austin State University (undergraduate degree), Thurgood Marshall School of Law (first law degree), and Georgetown University Law Center (advanced law degree). In 1996, I finally completed my formal education and thought my days in a classroom were officially behind me. Nothing could have been further from the truth.

After graduating from Georgetown, I landed my first full-time job as a tax adviser in a "Big Six" accounting firm in Houston. On the first day of work, I felt genuinely excited and proud of my prior accomplishments and everything that I had to offer my new employer. But as soon as I received my first challenging work assignment, my self-confidence and pride were quickly replaced with overwhelming feelings of insecurity and incompetence. Even though I was no longer sitting in a classroom, my education was far from over. Like most people at the beginning of their new career, my first days were filled with plenty of on-the-job training and anxiety as I learned the ropes.

As my career progressed, I finally started to regain my confidence. After cutting my teeth at the accounting firm, I practiced tax law for a brief time at a medium-sized law firm in Amarillo before finally landing my current (full-time) job as an in-house tax attorney for a Fortune 500 corporation.

Although my new career as a tax attorney was both challenging and rewarding, something seemed to be missing. Soon, I felt the urge to get back into the classroom—but this time I wanted to sit on the other side of the teacher's desk. So I applied for adjunct teaching positions at various community colleges. A few years later, I finally landed my current (part-time) job as an adjunct faculty member at a large community college in Texas. My first teaching assignment was a Saturday morning Business Law class in the fall of 2001, and I was so excited!

Having taught classes at the same community college for 15 years and attended college and graduate school for the eight years prior to that, I am confident that I have accumulated sufficient experience in the classroom to know what it takes to be an effective college instructor.[1] This book is intended to share my insights and give you 44 practical tips that will help you teach fun and engaging college classes.

So how do you know whether your teaching methods and strategies are successful? Obviously, you're doing things right if your students are actively engaging in and mastering the course materials. Fortunately, there are numerous ways to measure your students' mastery of course materials, including their final course grades, daily grades (especially for those students who don't test well), attendance records, retention rates (how many students completed the entire course and earned a grade), graduation rates, and so on. But perhaps the most convincing

---

[1] For purposes of this book, the term "college instructor" is used broadly and intended to include all college and university level teaching positions, whether tenure or non-tenure track.

way to measure student learning is to directly ask them what they think about their instructor and the teaching methods used in the course. To that end, most colleges and universities administer anonymous course evaluations to all students near the end of each semester.

My students' course evaluations are usually filled with high praise for my frequent use of adult humor and unique teaching methods. These evaluations show a consistent pattern of excellent reviews from each of the 27 semesters (and counting) that I have taught thus far. Below is a sample of actual quotes (minus typos and grammatical errors) from my students as expressed on anonymous course evaluations during the past 15 years:

> **Fall 2001: Wonderful personality—excellent with the students. Knows the students and their interests. Truly enjoyable class! Will definitely take a course taught by him again.**

> **Fall 2002: You're doing a great job! I can tell you like teaching and you're very good at sparking the students' interests! Keep up the good work!**

> **Spring 2005: Mr. Kowis goes on my top ten teachers of my life list. He is great, wonderful, full of energy, and enjoys sharing his work and knowledge with us. He is by far one of the greatest teachers I have ever had. He has such energy, he speaks clearly and writes a lot, and he makes all of us feel special and has us all participate. He also calls us all by name and treats each of us as an individual. There is a lot of class participation and fun.**

> **Spring 2006: Kowis enjoys his subject and enjoys teaching—very effective.**

> **Fall 2007: He is one of the best TEACHERS I have ever had. Getting the information to make sense is the best method, and Mr. Kowis makes sure that we understand. I am very lucky to have him as a teacher.**

Fall 2008: We need more professors like this at every institution.

Spring 2009: I like your unusual style of teaching. I really enjoyed your class. I hope to get more teachers like you, especially in the science department.

Fall 2010: By far my favorite professor. I wish every professor taught like Mr. Kowis.

Spring 2011: By far, absolutely the best teacher I have had at this college. (I have 60 credits taken here.) The class was intellectually challenging, but fun and entertaining, and I definitely LEARNED everything about the subject.

Fall 2012: Excellent instructor. One of the best, if not the best instructor I have taken. He makes the class easy and understandable, although it's a difficult subject.

Fall 2013: Probably the best teacher I've ever taken at college. This guy needs a raise, promotion, or higher position. He knows what he's talking about and loves teaching.

Fall 2014: This is honestly one of the most enjoyable classes I've taken. He keeps the students engaged and does his best to break down complicated material for the students to grasp.

Spring 2015: There is a lot of material in the course; however, I believe that I will retain what I have learned by how the class is taught by Professor Kowis.

Spring 2016: I admire Mr. Kowis because he is willing to sacrifice time away from his family to teach others what he really enjoys. I have taken many courses in the past, but this is the only time I have seen a professor who is passionate about his work and teaches with such enthusiasm. Thank you!

My sense of humor and unconventional teaching style have also caught the attention of students not enrolled in my class. For example, I was in the middle of a three-hour night class when a young man peered into my classroom from the hallway. The door was wide open (as is customary when I'm teaching), and the young man seemed intrigued by the lively lecture and playful banter between me and my students. Although it's not uncommon for my former students to pop their heads into class during a lecture and say hello, I didn't recognize this particular student. So I stopped the lecture and asked whether I could help him. His response was both surprising and heartwarming. He simply asked whether he could join the class because it "sounds like fun." I smiled and said that I'd be happy to have him join my class next semester and explained that the course I teach is called Business Law.

Truth be told, this wasn't the first time that strangers have hung around my classroom door to hear a little bit of my off-the-wall lectures and corny jokes. If my unorthodox teaching style can grab the attention of total strangers, it should have an even greater effect on my own students.

So who is this book intended to help? If you've ever wondered what it's like to teach a fun and engaging college class, this book is for YOU. If you're a current college instructor who is looking for practical tips to significantly increase your students' attention and engagement in classroom discussions, this book is DEFINITELY for you. As a friendly warning, this book does contain some adult humor, juvenile pranks and occasional curse words. If that's not your cup of tea, this book is probably not for you. So without further ado, let us begin...

PART 1

DOs and DONTs

Chapter 1: Recipe for Successful Student Engagement

The instructor teaches the subject in a way that makes it entertaining and fun for the whole class, and it makes me feel like I've learned something. I think many teachers need to teach in his style of teaching.

—Anonymous student evaluation from Spring 2012

Any successful chef will tell you that a delicious meal is no accident. Every great meal starts with a great recipe as well as the finest ingredients. That is no different for an effective college instructor whose chief mission is to fully engage her students in the course materials. This recipe calls for the following essential ingredients:

- 1 part Entertainer (to grab your students' attention),

- 1 part Coach (to inspire your students to work hard),

- 2 parts Parent (to show you care about your students' success),

- 1 part Law Professor (to apply the Socratic-lite method), and

- 1 part Classroom Teacher (to give effective lectures).

To complete the recipe, simply combine the above ingredients into a college instructor and apply to a classroom full of eager students. Bon appétit!

The above recipe may sound over-simplistic, but it captures the essence of what it takes for college instructors to successfully engage their students. The following pages will help you successfully achieve this and more.

Before we jump into the five ingredients, here are a few notes to consider: First, you will notice that the recipe calls for two parts Parent and only one part of the other ingredients. The reason for this disparity is that the single *most important* ingredient is showing that you genuinely care about your students and their success in the classroom. Second, note that the five ingredients have been grouped into two main topics. The first three ingredients (Entertainer, Coach, and Parent) relate to the connection between the instructor and her students, and the latter two ingredients (Law Professor and Classroom Teacher) relate to the instructor's method of classroom instruction. Hence, the chapters covering the first three ingredients are grouped into Part II of this book while the latter two ingredients comprise Part III. Finally, Chapter 2 will share some important (and sometimes embarrassing) lessons that I have learned the hard way. I include them here in the hope of sparing you from the same mistakes.

Chapter 2: What NOT to Do!

He should avoid inappropriate jokes. Sometimes I think his jokes are too inappropriate and don't really make me laugh. But for most of the time, he is funny.

—Anonymous student evaluation from Fall 2012

Anyone who has ever started a new job can attest to the fact that mistakes will happen as you learn the ropes of your new position. When that happens, the key is to learn from your mistakes and to move forward with your head held high. Despite my best efforts, I have made several mistakes in my teaching career, especially early on. One important lesson that I learned is that some tactics or behaviors, no matter how well intended, can alienate students or otherwise discourage them from fully participating in class. Below is a list of the eight most interesting (read, "embarrassing") no-nos that I have committed and the lessons I learned from each.

1) Don't make fun of students' names.
2) Don't keep your class late.
3) Don't be vulgar.
4) Don't use demeaning language toward a student.
5) Don't assume unprepared students are lazy.
6) Don't argue with students in class.
7) Don't allow students to dominate class.
8) Don't pass gas on students!

PRO TIP 1: Don't Make Fun of Students' Names (Unless You Know Them Well)

As discussed more fully in Chapter 3, one important goal for a successful college instructor is to maximize student attention and engagement. This goal can be achieved by keeping class interactions light-hearted and fun as often as possible. However, this should not be accomplished at the expense of humiliating or offending any particular student. To that end, an instructor should avoid jokes that might be perceived as personal attacks, including making fun of students' names.

This rule seems obvious enough, but I learned it the hard way while playing an icebreaker game during the first class of one particular semester. When called upon, one student announced to the class that her name was Candice, but she preferred to be called Candy. Without giving it a second thought, I jokingly asked if Candy was her stripper name. The class broke out laughing (as they often did during this icebreaker game), and Candy seemed to take the joke in stride. However, she didn't return to class the following week. When I tried contacting her to make sure that everything was okay and that she intended to remain in the course, Candy never responded. Soon thereafter, she dropped the class. Though it's not uncommon for a few students to drop a class during the first few weeks of each semester (which can happen for any number of reasons), I'm still haunted by the possibility that she might have withdrawn from class because of my joke.[2]

On the other hand, I once had a witty African American student named De'Andre Guin who told the class that his old nickname was "Chocolate Drop." This was about halfway through the semester when he revealed this funny nickname, and I knew both De'Andre and the rest of the class quite well by

---

[2] If by chance Candy is reading this book, I would like to sincerely apologize if my joke upset her, and also to let her know that I will never make fun of another student's name (at least not unless I know the student well enough to be sure that it won't cause offense).

then. Every class has its own personality, and this particular one was fun and lively. These students were all good-natured and thoroughly appreciated a hearty laugh from time to time. So the next time De'Andre walked into the classroom, I smiled at him and said, "Hello Chocolate Pudding!" The following week it was "Chocolate Chip," then "Lemon Drop," "Testicle Drop," etc. Each time, De'Andre and the entire class ate it up, and soon others joined in on the fun by making up their own nicknames for De'Andre. He was very good-natured about this ribbing and seemed to love the attention. One of De'Andre's classmates gave him a giant five-pound chocolate bar on the last class of the semester in honor of his unique nickname. De'Andre thought the gift was hilarious, and said his young kids would enjoy eating it.[3]

A little good-natured ribbing is usually well received by my students, but if you don't feel comfortable teasing your students, then you should find an alternative method of showing that you care about them. See Chapter 5 for more ideas.

> *Lesson learned*: Don't make fun of students' names unless you know them well enough to be certain that they won't take personal offense.

---

[3] De'Andre and I remain good friends to this day. His quick wit, outgoing personality, and big sense of humor made that particular class very enjoyable for me and my students.

PRO TIP 2: Don't Keep Your Class Late

When I first began teaching, I had an annoying habit of keeping the class well after the final bell rang so I could finish the lecture and administer a daily quiz. It quickly became obvious that my students didn't like staying late and that many of them had legitimate reasons to leave class on time. Some had to catch a ride home from a friend who was waiting for them in the parking lot. Others needed to relieve a babysitter who was watching their kids or an elderly parent. Again and again, they complained on their course evaluations about my bad habit of keeping them late. In fact, this was by far the most common complaint that I received during the early years of my teaching career.

This problem was not easy to solve. On one hand, I wanted to cover all of the key parts of the lectures that I planned, but I also wanted to continue giving daily quizzes as a way of summarizing the key materials and rewarding students who attended class. Upon reflection, I discovered that class ran late because I took the time to answer so many questions from my students. Of course I didn't want to discourage this behavior because we all know that vibrant class participation is crucial to the learning process. But when an instructor keeps the class late, students tend to think their personal time isn't being respected, and that's certainly not the impression we want to make.

To resolve this problem, I decided to continue covering all of the pertinent parts of the lecture and also to allow my students to ask any and all relevant questions they may have during class. But doing these two things does not always leave enough time to take the daily quiz before the bell rings. Rather than skipping the quiz, I decided to simply hand it out along with the correct answers and thereby reward all students in attendance with a 100 grade on the quiz. The only downside to this solution is that students miss the educational benefits of taking the daily quiz while the material is still fresh on their minds. On the bright side, they can use the quizzes to study for the next test.

Despite using this compromise for many semesters, I still occasionally fail to dismiss class on time. But when it happens now, I only extend the class period by an extra five or ten minutes at most.

> *Lesson learned:* Don't keep students in class after the final bell rings.

> **Spring 2002: My biggest complaint is not letting us out on time. My family has worried about me coming home so late. We have been held as late as 30 minutes. This would not be a big deal to me if there wasn't a quiz at the end of class that will affect your grade if you choose to leave early.**

> **Spring 2005: Most nights we were kept 30 minutes or more after scheduled class time. There was a lot of material to cover, but I feel this could have hurt class morale.**

> **Fall 2006: Night classes are tough. When we start to go over our time limit, we get tired. We stop focusing on what you are teaching. No one really gets the info when we are cramming it in.**

> **Spring 2007: Going past 9 pm every time kinda sucks. We have to take a quiz at the end, so we have to stay. Three hours is already a long time to be in a class-room.**

PRO TIP 3: Don't Be Vulgar

One of the biggest challenges of teaching a three-hour night class is keeping your students interested and engaged throughout the entire class. After working or attending school all day, many night students are exhausted and prone to falling asleep or daydreaming if given half a chance. As suggested in Chapter 3, one effective tip for keeping your students' attention is to sporadically interject colorful language into the lecture, including mild curse words or adult topics as a way to spice up an otherwise boring example. Using a little "French" language from time to time is a very effective tool for waking up your students, especially when you do so to break up a long technical discussion that otherwise would put them to sleep.

However, using colorful language in class is not without risks. For example, the instructor must avoid cursing in a manner that is offensive or derogatory toward the class. Insulted or irate students are not likely to give the instructor their undivided attention. Also, you must not use swear words too frequently. If you cuss like a sailor in every class, the shock value will quickly wear off and lose its intended effect.

On one occasion, I got carried away during an animated lecture and foolishly let an F-bomb slip, something to the effect of "what the &#%@?" As soon as the word left my lips, I knew that I'd gone too far. As you can imagine, the class reacted with dropped jaws and blank stares. After a second or two, I broke the deafening silence with a big smile and an immediate and sincere apology of "Oops... my bad!" Luckily everyone laughed and no one seemed to take personal offense from my poor choice of words. If my F-bomb had been directed at the class or a particular student, it would have been unforgiveable by anyone's standards.

> *Lesson learned:* Save the F-bombs for the next heated argument with your obnoxious neighbor or for pillow talk with your sexy spouse.

Spring 2010: Very unprofessional because of perverted jokes and EXCESSIVE crude language.

Fall 2012: Mr. Kowis is sometimes crude in his attempt to make the class interesting.

PRO TIP 4: Don't Use Demeaning Language

As discussed in Chapter 3 below, I often come up with crazy examples in class to illustrate a point. I frequently include one or more of my students in the example in order to pique their interest and help them feel connected to the lecture. Once I included the name of a student sitting in the front row as part of an example and then asked whether she had certain legal rights after the example played out. Before answering the question, the student asked if she was "still the same" (meaning her rights and liabilities under the law were unchanged) as a result of the example. Without thinking, I jokingly replied, "Yep, you are still the same bus station skank that you've always been." I immediately realized that this joke might come across as a personal attack and explained that my remarks were only intended as a joke and that she was in no way a "skanky ho" in real life. Even though the joke got big laughs from the class and succeeded in grabbing their attention, it was made in poor taste and I instantly regretted it. Lucky for me, she just laughed it off.

Lesson learned: Teasing students in a friendly way is one thing, but never use demeaning or derogatory language toward a particular student.

Spring 2016: The jokes are funny, but can be mean. Try humor that isn't at the expense of another.

PRO TIP 5: Don't Assume Unprepared Students Are Lazy

Early in my teaching career, I assumed the primary reason students came to class without reading the assigned chapters or failed a test was due to their laziness or lack of motivation. Without question, laziness is often the culprit. However, I eventually realized that some underperforming students have valid reasons for coming to class unprepared. Some college students have extremely heavy demands from their job, other classes (especially full-time students), and family commitments (such as raising young children or caring for an elderly parent). Other students may be suffering from a physical illness or enduring an unstable or unhealthy home life that makes it very difficult to concentrate and study.

The cold reality is that everyone has struggles in life and the grade that a student earns may or may not be his highest priority, and perhaps rightfully so. In fact, some students are perfectly content earning a "C" in the class provided it brings them one step closer to earning a college degree and finally beginning the new career they have always dreamed about.

> *Lesson learned*: Don't assume underperforming students are lazy and unmotivated.

PRO TIP 6: Don't Argue with Students in Class

Unfortunately, a Business Law course tends to bring out the "lawyer" in some students. In fact, it's not uncommon for some of my students to start an argument with me on particular points of law despite my vast experience as a tax attorney and Business Law instructor.

For example, a student once protested that his incorrect answer on a daily quiz was in fact correct. To explain the correct answer, I gave an analogy involving a car repair scenario. The student angrily claimed that I must not know anything about auto mechanics. My initial impulse was to puff out my chest and let it be known that I earned an "A" in high school auto mechanics, have successfully rebuilt car engines and transmissions in my garage, and still enjoy auto mechanics as a personal hobby. But before I spouted off, I took a deep breath and reminded myself that boasting about my superior mechanical knowledge wouldn't solve anything. Instead, I calmly told the student that he could insult me all that he wanted, but it wouldn't change the answer to the question. I also reminded him of the big picture, which is to say that I was only trying to help him understand the correct answer so he would be prepared for any similar questions on the upcoming exam. This response seemed to appease the student, and he stopped arguing.

Whenever students challenge you in front of the entire class, you should find a resolution that will allow your challengers to save face without giving the false impression that their arguments are correct. If it becomes apparent that a quick resolution is not possible, you should offer to discuss the matter during the next break or after class. The last thing you want to do is allow the student to escalate the argument to the point where your competence or authority is questioned in front of the entire class. If that happens, it might encourage other students to be disruptive, and the combative student might confuse the rest of the class by spouting off incorrect or irrelevant arguments.

Lesson learned: Don't lower yourself by engaging in a heated argument with a belligerent student. As Winston Churchill once said, "Never engage in a battle of wits with an unarmed man."

PRO TIP 7: Don't Allow Students to Dominate Class

When I was in college, I often found myself feeling frustrated when a handful of talkative students dominated class discussions on a routine basis. This situation may give the appearance that the teacher is playing favorites and the rest of the class is not welcome to answer questions or provide meaningful input.

As a college instructor, I make a point to call on everyone at least once during each class. When I pose a question to the entire class and multiple hands go up, I avoid selecting the same students over and over again. It's tempting to frequently call on your best students because they're likely to give the correct answer and then you can move on to the next lecture topic. However, you should remind yourself that the other students also paid their class tuition and deserve an equal chance to provide their input. Also, calling on a variety of students will help you gauge how well your class is grasping the course materials. If you find that your slower students are struggling with a particular topic, you can slow down and cover those topics in greater detail.

> *Lesson learned:* Call on a variety of students in each and every class.

> **Fall 2002: Gets all students involved, and allots each student time to answer the question instead of getting the answer from know-it-alls.**

PRO TIP 8: Don't Pass Gas on Students!

This may sound like an obvious no-no, but I learned this embarrassing lesson the hard way. During a ten-minute break in the middle of a three-hour night class, I was walking back from the restroom when I saw one of my students talking on his phone in the hallway. I had previously joked with this particular student in class many times, and he always seemed to enjoy my playful banter and juvenile sense of humor. For whatever reason, I suddenly thought it would be humorous to stop in front of this student and pass gas in a loud, obnoxious manner while he was still talking on the phone. You can imagine the look on his face as he witnessed his "distinguished and scholarly" college instructor cut the cheese right next to him. I laughed out loud and quickly walked into the classroom. A few seconds later, the bewildered student returned to the classroom and announced to the entire class, "I can't believe that Mr. Kowis just farted on me!" His classmates broke into hysterical laughter, and I was red-faced for the next five minutes. What I thought was going to be a funny, juvenile prank between just us guys turned into public humiliation and another hard lesson learned.

> *Lesson learned*: What else can be said? Don't pass gas on your students!

PART II

Connecting with Students

Chapter 3: Entertainer

He made a boring course into something that I had and would pay attention to. I only fell asleep once!

—Anonymous student evaluation from Spring 2016

I have observed that the average college student's attention span has shrunk significantly over the years and is now at an all-time low. This is no surprise given that virtually all books, movies, songs, and videos are instantly accessible to the public via a mobile device such as a cellphone, tablet, or laptop. In addition to these distractions, there is nothing that will shorten a college student's attention span further than a lifeless, boring, and monotone lecture, especially if the particular topic is something that does not personally interest or entertain the student.

One effective method for college instructors to grab and retain their students' attention and actively engage their minds in the topic at hand is to be an entertainer. Creating an entertaining and engaging learning environment is especially critical if you're teaching an off-hour class (e.g., a night class or an early morning class) or a dry subject matter (e.g., contract law or elements of the periodic table).

To entertain today's college student, you should apply some or all of the following tips in your classroom:

1) Tell adult jokes and funny stories.

2) Curse occasionally.

3) Wear a zany hat or costume.

4) Use crazy examples.

5) Sing and dance.

6) Give praise often.

7) Perform skits.

8) Do magic tricks.

9) Impersonate celebrities.

10) Be energetic.

Before we delve into the details of each tip, I must caution that what works well for me might not work for all instructors. I happen to have an outgoing personality and feel perfectly comfortable carrying on a conversation with others, including strangers. I also enjoy the art of storytelling, especially if the story is humorous or outrageous. If you're uncomfortable telling jokes or humorous stories to your class, chances are that it will show and your students won't enjoy it. So feel free to skip any of these tips if they don't mesh with your personality. The worst thing you can do is to act like someone you are not and come across as scripted or fake. In any case, it is my sincere hope that all instructors (including those with a dry or no sense of humor) can benefit from some of the tips in this book. The key message of this chapter is that your students will be much more engaged if you simply make an effort to loosen up and bring some levity to the class.

Now let's review each tip in greater detail.

Fall 2011: Prof. Kowis makes this subject interesting and not boring. This makes it much easier to learn the subject matter. To me, he is a brilliant professor!

Spring 2012: I know it sounds childish, but he makes learning fun. I looked forward to Wednesday nights because I always had a good time learning everything there is to know about business law. Ask me ANYTHING! I had Professor Kowis!

Fall 2012: To me, law is a dry subject. But Mr. Kowis makes it very vivid for me to understand through examples and a fun atmosphere in class.

Fall 2013: He uses bizarre examples to help explain a certain situation. If you remember the example, you won't be able to forget the topic.

Spring 2014: Absolutely amazing professor!!! He uses humor by applying the subject matter to ludicrous and hypothetical situations as a method to keep his students actively learning and involved in his lectures. This is by far one of the best classes I've ever taken!

Spring 2015: The instructor has a very entertaining teaching style, and keeps everyone engaged.

PRO TIP 1: Tell Adult Jokes and Funny Stories

One of the first things I learned as a college freshmen was that many topics that were off-limits for discussion in a public high school classroom were now perfectly acceptable—and in many instances are encouraged. I was surprised to learn that college students are actually encouraged to voice their personal opinions on religion, politics, and other adult topics. Having grown up in the conservative South, this newfound freedom gave me a strong sense of empowerment.

In the spirit of academic freedom, I believe it is perfectly acceptable to interject a little spicy language and adult humor into the college classroom for the purpose of keeping students alert and providing a little levity to otherwise dry subjects. Simply put, you can't effectively teach anything to students who are asleep.

When I'm joking around with my students to keep them awake during their three-hour night class, a typical exchange might go something like this:

On the very first night of class, I usually greet the last few students who enter the classroom with "*Guten Tag!* Welcome to German 1301." At a minimum, this little prank results in a quizzical look or a smile from the students as they proceed to take their seats. Occasionally, an embarrassed student will make an abrupt turn toward the door followed by a nervous giggle from the rest of the class. One semester, I welcomed a student entering my class on the first night by saying, "Welcome to Sex Education 101." Without missing a beat, the thirty-something student replied, "Yes, finally!"

After the above prank, I usually write my name on the board and formally introduce myself to the class as Mr. Kowis. Then I give my students the option of calling me by other names, such as Professor, Instructor, Hey You, Carlos Danger—or as my wife likes to call me, Jackass. And then I caution the class against using that last nickname by reminding them that I will be the person assigning their final grades at the end of the semester.

This little joke usually breaks the ice and sets the tone for the entire semester.

When discussing the common law concepts of comparative negligence and contributory negligence, I often use a crazy story involving one of my students (preferably a big, burly male student) walking his beloved pet poodle Fifi across a busy six-lane highway during rush hour (obviously a negligent thing to do). This story also involves another student from class who is driving 110 mph in a red convertible Ferrari (complete with a dead hooker in the truck) on the same highway while snorting an eight ball of coke and texting on his phone (also a negligent act). Finally, I explain that Fifi accidentally gets run over by the Ferrari, and then ask one of my students to analyze how comparative negligence and contributory negligence would apply to this bizarre scenario.

Instead of using this over-the-top story involving two of my students, could I have used a simple, more realistic story involving two fictitious people acting negligently in some common way? Sure, but my students are much more likely to recall the amusing image come test time, especially if it involves a few students from class.

When discussing the concept of trade dress (a type of intellectual property that is associated with the unique overall appearance of a product or place of business), I often use an example that everyone can easily relate to. For example, I might mention the Hard Rock Café (a popular restaurant decorated with signed memorabilia from famous rock stars) or Sport Clips (a popular barbershop for men that is decorated in a unique sports theme and displays sporting events on multiple TVs located throughout the salon). When pressed for more examples of trade dress, I once gave a wild example of a sadism and masochism-themed restaurant with whips and chains on the walls, waitresses dressed in leather and spiked dog collars who beat the crap out of their customers after taking their orders for hamburgers. My students are not likely to forget this naughty example of trade dress.

When explaining the definition of "fiduciary relationship" as a relationship between two people involving a high degree of trust and loyalty, I will sometimes use the example of a vasectomy patient and his urologist. After all, I ask, "Who requires a higher degree of trust than the surgeon who's about to cut your junk?"

When discussing the requirement of serious intent in the context of forming a valid contract, I often ask a student to brief the famous case of *Lucy v. Zehmer*, 196 Va. 493 (1954). In this case, one legal issue is whether a purported agreement to sell a farm can be set aside based upon Mr. Zehmer's claim that he was just kidding about the sale of his farm to Mr. Lucy. In one particular class, I mistakenly referred to Lucy as a woman, and a student quickly corrected me. "Thank you for pointing out that Lucy has a penis," I quipped, "but I'm not sure if that is relevant to the legal issue at hand." My students cracked up during an otherwise boring discussion of this breach of contract case.

I've found that it's very beneficial to occasionally use self-deprecating humor or funny examples involving myself as the butt of the joke. Self-deprecating humor shows your students that you're easygoing, down-to-earth, and likeable. You don't want to come across as a pretentious jerk as that might create an environment where students are afraid to speak up or ask questions. Students are much less likely to participate in class discussions if they don't like or respect the instructor, can't relate to the instructor, or if they somehow feel unworthy of the instructor's time and attention.

For example, one embarrassing story that I occasionally share with my students involves the time I took my 18-month-old daughter to a class that uses music and games to develop the toddlers' fine motor skills and eye-hand coordination. Getting to this evening class on time was a challenge for me, and one particular night I found myself running late. When I finally got home after a long day at work, I quickly threw on an old pair of shorts and a comfortable T-shirt.

When the class began, the instructor asked the parents to sit cross-legged in a large circle with their child sitting on their lap. As the music played, we were instructed to move our child's hands and feet to the rhythm. Most of the parents were young mothers, and during the exercise, I noticed several moms checking me out. I remember thinking to myself, "Yep, I still got it!"

During the mid-class break, the children played on some equipment in the middle of the room while the parents sat on benches along the edges of the classroom. My wife walked up to me and said, "I really like your underwear." I looked down to discover that my old shorts had a gigantic hole in the crotch. So that's why all the moms were checking me out while we were sitting cross-legged in the circle! Instead of admiring my good looks and charm, they were wondering what kind of SICK PERVERT goes to a toddlers' class with a giant hole in the crotch of his shorts!

Here's another story that I sometimes share with my class: I was sitting near the rear of a large church during a very crowded Sunday morning service when a young mother and her five- or six-year-old child came in late and sat down in the pew in front of me. I noticed that the child was holding a Buzz Lightyear action figure from the popular *Toy Story* movies. Worried that the mother hadn't remembered to remove the batteries, I anxiously waited to see whether the toy would make noises when the child played with it. After ten minutes or so, I decided that the toy must have been turned off or the batteries were indeed removed. In the middle of the sermon, the priest briefly paused between sentences, and we suddenly heard the booming voice of Tim Allen saying, "To infinity and be-yoooooond!" The entire church burst into laughter and turned toward my general direction to look for the culprit. Much to my chagrin, the inattentive mother and her disruptive son immediately crouched down in their pew, and I felt the heavy gaze of everyone's stare. As you can imagine, my face turned three shades of red!

Embarrassing stories like these show students that you're only human and occasionally suffer from embarrassment like everyone else. A little humility goes a long way toward helping students relate to their instructor. If they can relate to you, they are much more likely to ask questions during class and approach you whenever they have problems. So, the funnier and more embarrassing the stories, the better.

Sometimes I throw in silly jokes too. For example, when discussing criminal assault and battery, I like to use an old joke intended for elementary kids. This little joke is intended to help my students remember that it's possible for a criminal to commit battery (an act involving offensive or harmful contact with another person) without also committing assault (an act causing fear or apprehension of battery) by sneaking up on the victim before the attack. The joke goes something like this:

QUESTION: How do you catch a unique rabbit?

ANSWER: Unique up on it. (bada bing!)

Yes, it's a childish joke. In any case, at least a few students will usually giggle at this corny joke while the rest of the class groans. More important, come test time my students are more likely remember the point I was trying to make if they will remember this silly joke.

When I teach criminal law, I like to call on a student to read aloud the definition of arson to the class. The textbook defines arson as the willful and malicious burning of another person's home. I usually cut off the student in mid-sentence and ask, "Did you just say skillful and delicious?" That joke is right out of the *Santa Clause 3* movie and never fails to get a laugh out of my class, especially from students who are parents of young kids.

Once, a student sitting in the front row placed an odd-looking electronic device on the desk. When I looked at him, he explained that it was an audio recorder and asked whether he could use it to record my lecture. I said yes and began my lecture. The next time I walked by the recorder, I picked it up and talked into it like a microphone. In my deepest Elvis Presley voice, I said, "Ahh, thank you. Thank you very much! This next song goes out to all the sexy ladies in the audience." The students laughed, and I returned the recorder to the student's desk. With a smile, I told him that he might want to delete that part of the recording, and then I immediately continued with the lecture as if nothing had happened. When your students never know what wacky thing you might say or do next, it keeps them attentive and on their toes.

I also like to joke around with my class just before I give a major exam by announcing that there will be "No test today!" I immediately follow that up with the explanation, "Instead we will be having a celebration of knowledge [short pause] and some folks will be celebrating longer than others." This usually elicits a combination of laughs and moans from my students. I also ask the class whether they have any last-minute questions about the materials or perhaps some last-minute prayers. Then I like to quip that so long as there are tests given in school, there will always be prayer in school. With these jokes, my goal is to put my students at ease and reduce their test anxiety.

Speaking of major exams, I periodically announce to the class how much time is remaining. Once when they were only 30 minutes into a 90-minute test, I announced, "Only 15 minutes left... [pregnant pause] until *American Idol* begins! But you have a whole hour left to complete the exam." Okay, I'll admit that some of these jokes are intended for my own entertainment.

If you tell enough jokes, a few of them will inevitably flop. But this shouldn't discourage you from trying to be funny or amusing. When I tell a joke that doesn't get any response from my students, I often follow it up by saying, "That's okay, some of these jokes are just meant for me." It's best to not worry about whether a joke will bomb or not. The key is that you make an honest effort to entertain the class from time to time because it shows that you care about your students' enjoyment of the class.

Even if you don't have a funny bone in your body, there's no reason why you can't use funny movie clips during class lectures. For example, if you're teaching a lesson on criminal law or litigation, you could show the class a few relevant scenes from the 1992 classic *My Cousin Vinny*. If you're teaching a lesson on sexual harassment in the workplace, a few clips from *Anchorman: The Legend of Ron Burgundy* could do the trick. For a lesson on identity theft, consider a few scenes from *Identity Thief*. Even if you don't possess the comic genius of Will Ferrell or Melissa McCarthy, you can borrow a little of their humor for the purpose of making your lectures more interesting and entertaining.

> **Spring 2002: Keep up the good humor. It makes the students be more active in class.**

> **Spring 2005: I enjoy his class. He's very goofy, which makes it more fun.**

> **Spring 2006: He also makes dorky comments about the material, but I remember the comments because they are so dorky.**

> **Fall 2007: He's funny and entertaining, while hitting the points of the lesson with various stories/cases for the class.**

> **Fall 2009: He keeps you involved and keeps lectures both educational and entertaining.**

> **Spring 2012: Professor Kowis is very funny and keeps the class laughing through a three-hour night class. He is the only reason I like business law.**

> **Fall 2013: His humor helps the information stick long after you left his class.**

> **Fall 2015: I have never seen anyone use humor more effectively. His class was a complete joy and I couldn't wait to see what he would say next.**

PRO TIP 2: Curse Occasionally

Using a little salty language can go a long way toward keeping college students awake and engaged during boring lectures. For example, if you notice some of your students zoning out or nodding off, feel free to use a few nonthreatening and non-demeaning curse words as part of a funny joke or crazy example to grab their attention. This is especially helpful for an early morning or late evening class.

As effective as this tool is for regaining students' attention, it is very important to avoid overusing it. As mentioned in Chapter 2 above, cursing in every lecture will soon become expected and no longer have the intended effect of surprising and waking up your students. Also, too much foul language could alienate students who might be offended by the frequent use of curse words. Remember, the goal of using colorful language is to grab your students' attention and engage them in class discussions, not to offend them.

Why should you use curse words in a college classroom? The hard reality is that communication in the classroom, or anywhere else for that matter, must be real to be effective. In other words, your lectures and class discussions must be relevant and realistic. For better or worse, today's society is filled with adult language. It only takes a quick browse through the internet, popular TV shows, movies, songs, and postings on your favorite social media to find explicit language and plenty of it. Even U.S. presidents and other high-ranking public officials have occasionally used colorful language in interviews and speeches to make their point. To eradicate all foul language from the college classroom would ignore reality and be totally inconsistent with your students' daily interactions with their peers and the world around them.

If you decide to follow this tip, you should never direct your curse words at a specific student or any other person (famous or otherwise). Doing so poses a significant risk that you might offend students who think you're being disrespectful, and offended students tend to dampen the overall learning environment in your classroom. On the other hand, if you are careful to use explicit language sparingly and never use it to demean or belittle anyone, the risk of offending your students should be minimal.

Students tend to be more receptive to colorful language if they clearly understand that their instructor's sole intent is to grab their attention and keep them awake during class. For that reason, you should make this intention known to the class the first time or two that you use adult language.

Admittedly, my intentional use of explicit language probably flies in the face of conventional classroom etiquette. The trick is to always be respectful and avoid making anyone uncomfortable when doing so. Just like Aretha Franklin, college students demand respect, and they deserve it too. To be respectful, the occasional swear word should be used only in jest and OBVIOUSLY in jest. It should be directed at no one in particular, especially no one in the classroom (unless you want to make fun of yourself, of course). The goal is to amuse and awaken your students, not offend them.

With that said, you should not restrict your language solely to spare the feelings of a few irrational or overly sensitive college students who forbid anyone in their presence from uttering any words they may find offensive. For example, some college students in Missouri have gone so far as to create "safe spaces" on campus where students are not allowed to freely express their personal viewpoints if they are counter to popular views. Some people refer to the attempt by an overly sensitive person to silence another person who expresses unpopular views and language as "political correctness." I consider this an unnecessary restriction on freedom of speech that has no place on a college campus. The free expression of ideas should be encouraged in the college classroom, even if that means some students may be exposed to ideas that they strongly disagree with or feel uncomfortable discussing. After all, the freedom to openly exchange different viewpoints often leads students to greater knowledge and a broader perspective. Furthermore, the potential benefits of grabbing your students' attention and helping them relate to the subject matter being discussed far outweigh the potential hurt feelings of an overly sensitive student or two. In other words, if you limit your language and lecture topics to appease the most-sensitive students in your class, you will end up teaching a very dry, straight-laced class where your students constantly struggle to stay awake and engaged. This is a lousy trade-off in my opinion.

Finally, you should always adhere to your college's policies on classroom behavior and decorum. Certainly, the occasional use of colorful language and adult jokes won't be well-received on all college campuses. For example, some religious universities may strictly forbid or strongly discourage its faculty and staff from using foul language on campus no matter how infrequently they are used, how innocuous the words may seem in their context, or how well-meaning the speaker may be. At many colleges, the stated policy is to balance your academic freedom with your students' *reasonable* sensitivities. This policy makes perfect sense and should be followed at every college in my opinion.

> **Spring 2015: The instructor makes everyone feel very comfortable participating in class.**
>
> **Spring 2016: Thanks for everything, Mr. Kowis!! I really enjoyed this course because of you. I don't really like law stuff. Wish teachers were more like you! PS - I love that you cuss!**

PRO TIP 3: Wear a Zany Hat or Costume

To grab your students' attention, you can wear a zany hat or costume that relates to the lecture topic. Mr. Scott, my high school English teacher, used this technique with great effect. He would read a passage from *The Canterbury Tales* while strumming a lyre and wearing a purple crushed velvet blazer and a medieval helmet. More than a quarter-century has passed, yet I still remember how much our entire class enjoyed those lessons. When he was dressed as one of Chaucer's pilgrims or Hamlet, he definitely made us want to listen to his every word.

If you're teaching a Texas history course, consider dressing in buckskins and addressing your students as if you were General Sam Houston telling your troops to remember the Alamo before they marched into the Battle of San Jacinto. If you're teaching an astronomy class, why not dress as Galileo and reenact the debate from the *Dialogue Concerning the Two Chief World Systems* between Salviati, Sagredo, and Simplicio? This kind of creative and dynamic teaching can bring any subject to life.

PRO TIP 4: Use Crazy Examples

Another effective tip for grabbing the attention of your students and helping them retain information is to use crazy examples to illustrate your points. The more outlandish the example, the more effective it is. Below are a few examples.

When discussing the topic of assault and battery, I often give the example of two lifelong friends who grew up living next door to each another. Rather than using random names for the friends in this example, I pick the names of two male students from the class. Let's call them Neal and Bob. In the example, Neal and Bob often play a game called slug bug, the object of which is to punch the other person first whenever they spot a Volkswagen Beetle. While these two friends are attaching Christmas lights to the outside of a house, Neal is on top of a tall ladder in the driveway and Bob is holding the ladder steady from the ground. A Beetle drives down the street, and Bob instinctively reaches up and punches Neal... [dramatic pause] right in the ol' BALL SACK and then yells, "slug bug!" Neal falls off the ladder and breaks his arm on the concrete driveway below. I use this ridiculous example to show that assault and battery can occur despite the lack of an evil motive by the aggressor. In this example, the boys are best friends and harbor no ill will toward one another. This nutty example (pardon the pun) usually gets big laughs. They laugh even louder if I follow it up by making a nervous reference to the open classroom door and expressing my sincere hope that the dean didn't just walk by and overhear me saying "ball sack."

Rather than using the outlandish example above, I could have simply stated that "boy number one" intentionally struck "boy number two" in the arm as part of a friendly game, but where is the humor or entertainment value in that? More important, do you think your students are more likely to recall this boring story or the absurd example above come test time?

Here's another silly example that I've used during class discussions of contract law. President Obama offers a million-dollar cash reward to any U.S. citizen who can bring back the head of Osama bin Laden. Despite wide media coverage, a U.S. citizen named Joe is out of the country and doesn't hear the offer. At that time, Joe is in Afghanistan enjoying his favorite hobby of spelunking. (Spelunking, I explain, is one of those interesting words that sounds dirty but isn't. It simply means to explore caves.) Anyway, Joe is spelunking in Afghanistan when he happens upon Osama's cave. In my most ridiculous "Osama" and "Joe" voices, I act out the following scene:

> JOE: [in a deep, sensuous voice] Mmmm. I love me some spelunking! There is just something about exploring another man's dark, musky-scented cave. It is so moist and warm in here. So deep too. Ahhh!
>
> OSAMA: [in a maniacal, foreign accent] Hey, what are you doing exploring my man-cave? Oh, that is just wroooooong! You are not allowed in here. Leave at once!
>
> JOE: Wait a minute... hold the phone. I know you. You're that evil terrorist who hates America. I can't stand you!

After the above exchange, I explain that Joe kills Osama and brings his head back to the White House as a gift for the president. Then I ask the class whether Joe is legally entitled to receive the million-dollar reward based upon the president's prior offer. [4] The above example is over-the-top and has elements of sexual innuendo, which is exactly the kind of crazy example that students are likely to recall during their next exam.

Here's yet another loony illustration that I sometimes use, this time when discussing a sole proprietorship business model. Before discussing the example, I randomly select two male students from the class. Let's assume I picked Neal and Bob again. Bob sells miniature gourmet hot dogs at a popular hot dog stand. Every weekend, Bob sets up his hot dog stand on the same corner of a busy intersection in Montrose (a diverse

---

[4] The correct answer is that Joe is not entitled to receive the reward under common law principles because a valid offer must be effectively communicated from the offeror to the offeree and here the president's offer was not effectively communicated to Joe.

neighborhood known for its gay and lesbian scene). He calls the hot dog stand "Bob's Teeny Wienies." His business is popular and customers come from miles around to eat Bob's delicious wieners. His biggest customer is Neal, who often says, "Mmmm... I just can't get enough of Bob's wieners in my mouth! They are so warm and tasty." The obvious sexual innuendo in this silly example usually makes the entire class laugh out loud. Usually, the two male students included in the above example are laughing the loudest.

> **Spring 2007: He has great examples. It really helps to remember the material. He's doing a great job. Thanks for a really great teacher finally!!**

> **Spring 2009: His weird sense of humor is the only reason I stay awake in class. He comes up with weird, sometimes aggressive examples that make me laugh so hard. The reason I remembered most of the questions on a test was because I remembered a joke that he said.**

> **Fall 2011: Loved the class, the examples are the best.**

> **Spring 2013: Teaches in a way that you remember. A lot of examples and funny scenarios that you can't help but recall when taking a test.**

> **Spring 2016: I really enjoyed Mr. Kowis' wild, crazy examples. They are very extreme and unforgettable, which makes it easier to learn and remember.**

PRO TIP 5: Sing and Dance

Outside of theater and dance classes, most college instructors don't sing or dance during class. Such a rarity would no doubt be a memorable and entertaining moment, especially if you're a poor singer or dancer. That's EXACTLY why you should perform an occasional song or dance routine for your class!

For example, when I discuss the Statute of Frauds, I usually ask the class for the five types of contracts subject to this common law rule. My students are usually able to list at least a few of them with the aid of their textbook. When they need help finishing the list, I usually give them a little clue by breaking into the opening lines from "Gold Digger," the 2005 hit song by Kanye West and Jamie Foxx. The irony is that I am a horrible, horrible singer. My singing talent is best described as somewhere between "Karaoke newbie" and "OMG, is someone dying?"[5] In any case, I'm willing to make a complete fool of myself because one of the lines from that old song refers to a pre-nup. Invariably, at least one student will recognize the song and figure out that the answer I'm looking for is "prenuptial agreement."

When the song "Gangnam Style" first became popular in 2012, I occasionally sang the catchy tune and did a few of the famous dance moves from the video just to kick off my class. It was a great way to add a little levity and wake up my students, who usually enter my night class in an exhausted state of mind after a long day of work or school.

When I call on a student in class for an answer and he doesn't know the correct answer, I usually instruct the student to search for the answer in the textbook. To fill the 30 seconds or so that it takes the student to flip through the pages and find the answer, I occasionally break out a rendition of whatever song and dance routine happens to be popular at the time—

---

[5] Believe it or not, a student once asked me to sing it again so she could record the performance on her phone and upload it to YouTube. Of course, I declined because I've already suffered enough public humiliation in class.

recently, Silento's "Watch Me (Whip/Nae Nae)." Of course, my obvious lack of talent as either a singer or dancer made my performance all the more enjoyable for my students.[6]

As a friendly word of caution, please be aware that anything embarrassing that you say or do in class may eventually reach the ears of your coworkers. For example, a fellow instructor recently asked to borrow my key card so he could get into the faculty offices. When he returned with my key, he said that we had a mutual student that semester. Apparently, our mutual student told this faculty member that I sometime discuss wild stories in class such as scenarios involving dead hookers and an eight ball of coke. I was stunned and didn't know how to respond. All I could do was put on a big smile and say, "Whaaaaaaat?" The other faculty member laughed and said that he just wanted to tell me to keep up the good work. Since that day, he always asks me if I'm covering dead hookers and cocaine in today's lecture.

---

[6] Thankfully, I have a teenage son to teach me these dance moves.

PRO TIP 6: Give Praise Often

Most college students are under enough stress without their instructor weighing them down further with a negative attitude or constant criticisms. Without a doubt, students are prone to be less attentive if they are feeling down or preoccupied with their daily problems. If you want to motivate and engage your students, you must praise them often and be a beacon of hope to your entire class.

So exactly how do you do that? First, you start the class with a positive comment, such as "It's so great to see your smiling faces today" or "I've been looking forward to this class all week." Then continue to say encouraging words throughout the class period. That is not to say that you should sugarcoat real problems that arise during the semester or give false praise to lazy or misbehaving students. However, you should make a concerted effort to say something positive about each student throughout the semester. Saying something as simple as "I'm so glad to be here with you guys and gals tonight because this is going to be a fun class!" might be enough to get a student out of a funk. It's important to cheer them up and remind them that they are talented and you expect them to be successful in your class.

You might be thinking the above advice is easier said than done. College instructors are people, and like all people we occasionally have bad days too. Just like my students, I often walk into class feeling exhausted and overwhelmed after a long hard day at my day job. To perk myself up, I usually refocus my thoughts on how much I truly love to teach and how much I have been looking forward to teaching class all week.

As the old saying goes, "If you love your job, you will never work a day in your life." Regardless of what kind of day I'm having, teaching class always feels like a mini-vacation from the nonstop demands of my day job and busy home life. When I'm tired, I remind myself of how lucky I am to have the opportunity to teach college students and help them fulfill their journey to a better job or career.

Fall 2006: Makes a dull subject interesting, creative, and upbeat.

Fall 2007: This is the best instructor I've had in a long time. He's a master at making sure we understand the subject and has a great positive attitude.

Spring 2008: He is a great teacher. He puts a lot of enthusiasm into each class and covers all the material in a very effective way.

Fall 2009: Keeps it interesting with his humor and upbeat attitude.

Spring 2013: Very enthusiastic, knows the material and is happy to teach it.

PRO TIP 7: Perform Skits

In my Business Law class, I frequently discuss important cases that are covered in the textbook. With the help of my students, I summarize or "brief" the key facts and legal issues of each assigned case on the whiteboard. Briefing cases is a useful tool used to sharpen law students' critical thinking skills. This exercise requires them to break down a particular court case into important categories, including the case name, relevant facts, the legal issue, the court's decision, and its rationale. The same exercise can also apply to any legal situation by separating it into similar categories. In the process of briefing the assigned case or legal situation, students must identify the relevant legal issues and apply the correct rule of law to reach the logical conclusion.

One of the cases that we brief in my Business Law class is the famous *Palsgraf v. Long Island Rail Road Company*, 248 N.Y. 339 (1928). This personal injury case involves an unexpected explosion of fireworks near a train depot that resulted in injuries to Ms. Palsgraf when a large scale fell on her while she was standing at the far end of the train platform. After we brief this case on the board, I select a handful of students to act out the key events of the case. On one side of the classroom, I ask a student to portray the train as it slowly pulls away from the depot, another student to portray a passenger trying to hop onboard the moving train, and a third student to portray the railroad guard as he tries to push the passenger aboard. On the opposite side of the classroom, I ask one student to portray Ms. Palsgraf and the other student to stand tall with outstretched arms so as to mimic the arms of a large scale.

Although this skit only takes a few minutes to organize and perform, it accomplishes two positive things. It gets my students up and out of their seats, and more important, it helps them visualize what led to Ms. Palsgraf's injuries. Generally, different students learn best by different methods, and acting out the facts of a case in a simple classroom skit should help those students who learn best by visual instruction.

As a practical matter, I only have sufficient time during the semester to perform one skit. If I had more time, I would perform skits to reenact all of the assigned cases. My hope is that students will use this one skit to visualize how the facts of this case unfolded and apply that same visualization technique to the following assigned cases. By applying this technique to the cases we study, students should better understand the facts and issues covered in each case.

Fall 2006: Examples and acting out situations helps me understand.

Fall 2006: Writing notes on the board as he goes along. Acting out examples. Quizzes.

PRO TIP 8: Do Magic Tricks

Another interesting way to liven up a class and grab students' attention is to occasionally perform a magic trick. I don't know any magic tricks, but I would happily apply this tip in my classes if I did. This tip should be most effective if you can somehow make the magic trick relevant to the topic you're discussing. For example, perhaps you could perform a simple disappearing act when teaching a chemistry lesson involving a chemical reaction that causes a chemical to "disappear" or transform into another chemical. Though it might sound juvenile or silly, this tip might create an interesting punctuation to an otherwise boring science lab.

PRO TIP 9: Impersonate Celebrities

Another effective way to grab your students' attention is to do impersonations of famous people. If you're like me and were not born with this talent, you can try to do an easy impersonation like Arnold Schwarzenegger. I occasionally use an Arnold voice when I'm telling a joke or cutting up with the class. It is not important that you sound exactly like the celebrity you're mimicking, as students will appreciate the simple fact that you made an honest effort to entertain them. Obviously, you should be careful to avoid impressions that could come across as demeaning or derogatory to a particular nationality or group. In any case, just have fun with it and your students will most likely have fun too.

PRO TIP 10: Be Energetic

In most exercise videos, the fitness trainer leading the workout session tends to be extremely energetic and enthusiastic. Similarly, athletic coaches typically exhibit an abundance of energy and passion when they coach their players. The reason for this is quite simple: all trainers and coaches want to inspire their group to perform at their best level and stay focused on the tasks at hand.

Likewise, motivational speakers often project tons of enthusiasm and energy when they address their audience. Take for example the famous *Saturday Night Live* skit starring the late Chris Farley. In this skit, he portrayed motivational speaker Matt Foley, who was hired by a concerned father to impart some words of wisdom to his two teenagers about the dangers of illegal drug use. In a booming voice, Chris Farley lets the teens know that bad decisions such as illegal drug use will only lead to "... a steady diet of government cheese and LIVING IN A VAN DOWN BY THE RIVER!" Farley ends the sketch by accidentally falling onto a coffee table, which disintegrates into a thousand pieces. It's comedy gold! Most motivational speakers are not quite as hilarious as this Matt Foley character, but they often use energetic voices and lively personalities just the same.

The college classroom is no different than an exercise video, football practice, or motivational speech in that the instructor is responsible for motivating their students to work hard, pay attention, and stay focused on the topics being discussed. You can accomplish this by exhibiting genuine passion and enthusiasm for the topics that you teach. No matter how knowledgeable and compassionate you may feel on the inside, you won't engage your students if you speak in a boring, monotonous voice.

> **Fall 2002: This was my second attempt at this class, and I'm extremely glad I got him for a teacher because this course can be extremely dry and he tried to make it as lively as possible.**

Spring 2008: His excitement is great. It makes me want to listen more to understand what he is teaching.

Spring 2009: I like that he is energetic. He makes three hours go by pretty fast.

Fall 2009: "Very engaging, energetic, loves material and excites students about it."

Fall 2011: His energy and entertaining way of presenting the material keeps the class interactive and gets all the students involved.

Spring 2013: Very animated. Makes the class fun.

Fall 2013: Mr. Kowis is very passionate about this subject and it shows. Very unique teaching method which I enjoyed very much, and I probably would not have done as well had it not been for his enthusiasm.

Fall 2014: Professor Kowis is very animated when he sees that students' attention is waning and this is very helpful.

Checklist and Action Items

Select at least three Pro Tips from this chapter that you are willing to implement in your classroom. Under each tip that you select, write down specific details of how you plan to implement the tip. If, for example, you have a funny story that you can tell that is relevant to a particular topic you are teaching, you could write a brief description of that story and the specific topic in your lecture that it relates to in the first section below.

<u>Ten Pro Tips for Being an Entertainer in the Classroom:</u>

1) Tell Adult Jokes and Funny Stories

_____

_____

_____

2) Occasionally Curse

_____

_____

_____

3) Wear a Zany Hat or Costume

_____

_____

_____

4) Use Crazy Examples

_____

_____

_____

5) Sing and Dance

_____

_____

_____

6) Give Praise Often

_____

_____

_____

7) Use Skits

_____

_____

_____

8) Perform Magic Tricks

_____

_____

_____

9) Impersonate Celebrities

_____

_____

_____

10) Be Energetic

_____

_____

_____

Chapter 4: Coach

~~~~~~

He is a great teacher when it comes to keeping your attention with stories and experiences of his own. He definitely keeps my attention, which I consider a high achievement when his students are usually full time employees and come at night, tired and exhausted from working all day, to further their education. I know that I am usually exhausted by the time I get to class, but he perks me right up and I get excited about learning.

—Anonymous student evaluation from Spring 2014

One common denominator of most championship football coaches is their ability to give a moving locker room speech that will motivate the entire team to perform at their very best. Similarly, successful college instructors must be able to inspire their students to perform at their maximum potential in the classroom. In fact, nothing you do or say in the classroom will have any lasting impact unless you can successfully motivate your students to work hard and apply themselves to their studies. To achieve this goal, you should apply the following six tips:

1) Correct distracting students.
2) Use real-world examples in lectures.
3) Show genuine interest in the course materials.
4) Demand communication.
5) Encourage students to speak with confidence.
6) Encourage students to think big.

PRO TIP 1: Correct Distracting Students

It seems the longer that I teach, the more frequently I notice my students doing things that distract their classmates. I'm not certain whether this observation is because I've become more keenly aware of such instances or whether this is a growing trend thanks to technology and the like. There are many student behaviors that can potentially distract others, the most common of which include the following situations:

A) Engaging in side conversations with classmates,

B) Sleeping in class,

C) Misusing mobile devices to surf the web, watch videos, or chat with others,

D) Consuming soda or food, and

E) Arriving late.

The good news is that many of these distracting behaviors can be eliminated or reduced with the implementation of appropriate classroom policies. Just be sure to include these policies in your syllabus and enforce them consistently. For example, I implemented an effective cellphone policy to be discussed in greater detail in Chapter 8. Since I began using this policy, I've had no more problems with students' phones ringing during class.

How to Address Side Conversations

I have noticed two types of side conversations involving my students. Some conversations involve a student asking a classmate to repeat something that I just said or discussing the possible answer to a question I have just posed to the entire class. These conversations are generally not harmful to the learning process so long as they are infrequent and not overly loud.

However, the second type of side conversation can be detrimental for both the talkative students and their classmates within earshot. This type of conversation involves two or more students discussing a topic that is completely unrelated to the lecture. Off-topic conversations are more likely to occur at the very beginning of class or immediately after a mid-class break, when the students are not yet focused on the class. When this happens, I usually stop talking and stare at the talkative students with a big smile on my face. Eventually, one or both of them will realize they are being disruptive and cease talking. At this point, I usually respond with a snarky comment, such as apologizing to the talkative students if my lecture interrupted an important conversation. "By all means, don't let my lecture get in your way. Please continue." Other times, I will join in their conversation, especially if they're talking about something silly or embarrassing.

If you do this a time or two, your talkative students should eventually get the hint to stop talking during class lectures. If they don't, you should pull them aside and have a private conversation with them at the break or after class. Remind them that their side conversations are unfair to their classmates who also paid to be in your class. This type of friendly warning usually solves the problem. If not, you may have to consider more drastic steps, including discipline measures. For example, you could ask them to leave class for the day the next time they are caught talking out of turn. In any case, be sure to follow your syllabus as to whatever discipline measures you decide to impose on your talkative students.

How to Address Sleeping Students

If a student falls asleep during class, I usually ignore this behavior the first time it happens unless the student is snoring loudly, drooling on the desk, or otherwise making a scene. Anyone can occasionally become sleep-deprived for a valid reason, especially during an early morning or night class. However, if this behavior becomes routine, you should have a private conversation to express your concern for the student's well-being and ask whether the student is feeling well. Due to privacy concerns, it is probably best if you don't specifically ask the student if there is a medical reason causing the frequent naps. Sometimes the student will voluntarily disclose that migraine headaches, side effects from medications, or other medical conditions are the cause for such sleepiness. In these situations, you should advise the student to consider seeking medical advice from a doctor.

If a student says that stress from a demanding job, a difficult family situation, or other responsibilities is interfering with his normal sleep patterns, you should advise the student to seek advice from one of the friendly counselors on campus.

On the other hand, if the student's frequent naps are the result of late-night parties or other irresponsible behavior, you should kindly ask her whether she is serious about being successful in the course. A student who is wasting time sleeping in class is obviously not getting anything out of the lectures and there is no point in attending class. In this situation, you should gently remind the student that, like anything else in life, she will get out of the class what she puts into it. If the habitual sleeper continues this destructive behavior, it will most likely result in failing grades. This is a sad situation, but all you can do is give a friendly warning about the possible consequences and let the student decide whether to change this behavior.

How to Address Technology Misuse

The unauthorized use of technology in the classroom has become more commonplace in the past decade as laptops, phones, and other mobile devices with internet capability have become ubiquitous. Often it's hard to decipher from the front of the classroom whether your students are using their mobile devices to take lecture notes, text their friends, or shop for a new purse on eBay. If they're acting like a typical student taking notes or reading a digital copy of the textbook, you can assume that they're probably not distracting their classmates. However, if you see a student laughing or grinning from ear to ear while staring at his phone screen during an otherwise boring part of the lecture, you can safely assume that student is probably not using technology to further his education. More important, you can assume that student's behavior is likely a distraction for his classmates. When this occurs, you should ask the student why he is smiling or laughing and then redirect him if necessary. But I'm happy to say that I've had to address these situations only on rare occasions. If you follow the tips in Chapter 3 for entertaining your students, you shouldn't have to deal with this situation too often.

How to Address Foodies

I've had a lot of students who eat or drink during my night class. This is especially likely to occur right after the mid-class break when students grab a salty snack or a diet soda from the vending machines just outside our classroom door. Most college students are adults and tend to eat and drink quietly except for the occasional noisy wrapper being opened or soda cap being twisted off. When this happens I rarely make a fuss. After all, it's perfectly understandable that some night students don't have enough time to eat dinner before class begins, especially if they are coming straight from a day job on the other side of town. I would rather they eat a snack and be able to focus on the lecture than be hungry and distracted. Sometimes I will be silly and ask if I can have a bite or if the student brought enough food for the entire class. But otherwise I just ignore it. Of course, you should check to see whether your college has a policy against students eating or drinking in the classroom.

How to Address Tardy Students

When students are late to class, all I ask is that they come in quietly and try not to distract their classmates. Nothing will grab the attention of students more than seeing or hearing a closed door suddenly open after class has already begun. Everyone wants to see who is coming in late. You can minimize this distraction by leaving the door wide open, which allows students to sneak in and out of the classroom like well-trained ninjas.

PRO TIP 2: Use Real-World Examples

To help your students understand the topics being discussed in class and commit the course materials to memory, you should tie the topic at hand to a real-life example. For example, copyright infringement should make more sense to your students if you discuss the latest copyright infringement lawsuit filed against a well-known pop star. These lawsuits seem to occur every year or so and are usually covered by national media outlets. For example, the estate of Marvin Gaye recently won a $7.4 million verdict against Robin Thicke and Pharrell Williams for copyright infringement regarding their hit song "Blurred Lines." Most college students are familiar with this popular song and it will help them recall what I've taught them about copyright infringement.

As another example, if you are generally discussing contract rights and liabilities, you could relate this topic to common contracts that your students most likely encounter in real life, such as contracts to purchase a home or car. Or if you're teaching Einstein's Theory of Relativity, you can explain that this is why time moves slower when you're with your relatives. Okay, that was just an old joke. But seriously, you could illustrate how this fundamental principle has tangible effects on the real world, such as how GPS satellite clocks would move slower relative to clocks on the surface of the earth if their velocity was not accounted for. This real-world application of Einstein's Theory is something that students will remember every time they open their Google Maps app.

It is also important to relate the topic at hand to both current events and past events so as to better reach younger students and older students alike. For example, if you are lecturing on acts of domestic terrorism in the United States, you could start by discussing the famous Oklahoma City bombing committed by Timothy McVeigh in 1995. Though many older students should recall this deadly attack, most young college students are probably unfamiliar with this horrific event. For that reason, you should also discuss a more recent attack that your younger students should know, such as the 2016 Orlando nightclub shooting committed by Omar Mateen.

Fall 2002: He makes up real-life situations to help you understand the material.

Spring 2005: He uses practical real-world examples. Everything we are learning can be applied to everyday life and he explains how.

Spring 2009: His outgoing personality makes the class. He gives real-life situations and makes them funny so it's easier to learn.

Fall 2012: He makes a dry subject fun and easier to understand by using everyday scenarios.

Spring 2015: Interesting and applicable stories pertaining to subject matter helps me connect Business Law with real life, both personally and professionally.

Spring 2016: He puts what we are learning into real world situations and that helps everyone remember what the law means and what exactly we are learning.

PRO TIP 3: Show Genuine Interest in the Course Materials

Teachers are more likely to hold the attention of their students if they genuinely care about the topic they're teaching. No one wants to sit in a classroom and watch a bored-out-of-her-mind instructor recite from a textbook in a monotone voice with no expression on her face. If the topic being taught is not interesting enough to excite the instructor, why should the students care either?

If you show sincere interest in the topic you're discussing, your passion should be contagious. Students are much more likely to get excited about what you're teaching if you're jumping around and making a big fuss about it.

> **Fall 2002: He gets the class involved and loves what he teaches. He enjoys our input and involves us in class discussions.**
>
> **Spring 2003: He is very interested in the material, explains things from many different angles, and he writes on the grease board, which helps to visually retain the material.**
>
> **Fall 2010: Very enthused teaching style keeps us interested.**
>
> **Fall 2012: The instructor is engaging and passionate about the subject matter. His enthusiasm is contagious!**

PRO TIP 4: Demand Communication

One life lesson that all students should learn is to communicate with others often and effectively. I expect my students to inform me as soon as possible whenever they are planning to miss a class, especially if they will miss a test and need to arrange to take it later. For privacy reasons, you should probably not ask your students for the particular reason why they will be absent. However, it is helpful if the student volunteers this information as it may give you a clue as to whether the student takes your class seriously or is just blowing it off.

Effective communication skills are critical for college students to learn because most students will someday be expected to use such those in the workplace. Communication skills also play a key role in their relationships with their family, spouses, and friends. So there is no reason why your students should not be expected to communicate in the classroom setting as well.

When students inform you of an absence ahead of time, you should advise them to make sure they read the chapters or materials scheduled to be covered during the missed class and get class notes from a fellow student afterward (if that is allowed in your class). If applicable, you should also arrange for a make-up test in the school's testing center.

PRO TIP 5: Encourage Students to Speak with Confidence

Another important life lesson that all college students should learn is how to speak with confidence, especially when they are giving a presentation or trying to persuade someone that their position is correct. To that end, you should encourage your students to speak with complete confidence whenever they answer one of your questions, even if they are unsure of their answer.

As a Business Law instructor, I often remind my class that a lawyer representing her client before a jury panel must speak with great confidence and conviction if she expects to be persuasive. The same is true when we're trying to persuade a college instructor, boss, spouse, or friend. To that end, you should correct your students whenever they start to answer your questions with nervous hesitation or a quivering voice. Whenever this occurs in my class, I ask the apprehensive student to pretend she is a lawyer in a capital murder trial and the client's life depends on her ability to persuade the jury of her client's innocence. To be persuasive, trial lawyers should always speak with complete confidence even when they're not entirely sure of the strength of their legal position. I expect the same level of confidence when my students speak in class.

PRO TIP 6: Encourage Students to Think Big

Many college students, especially community college students, walk into class with a narrow-minded perspective on life. Whether they were raised their whole life in a small town or came from a home with modest resources, it is crucial for students to open their minds to the unlimited possibilities that life has to offer. I often ask my students to name a grand item they want someday so I can use it in an example. Specifically, I might ask a student for his dream car or a business that he someday hopes to own. If the student selects a common car like a Honda Accord, I immediately respond by telling the student to think bigger and better, such as a canary yellow BMW convertible or a bright red Lamborghini. The idea is to spark an interest in the finer things in life and hopefully inspire the student to pursue lofty goals, such as owning his own business or vacation home in Hawaii, or becoming a world-renowned brain surgeon. Those interests and goals will never become a reality unless the student dares to dream big.

Checklist and Action Items

Select at least two Pro Tips from this chapter that you are willing to implement in your classroom. Under each tip that you select, write down specific details of how you plan to implement the tip. For example, perhaps you are interested in preventing distractions from students who come to class late. Under tip number one below, write a brief description of your idea for a new class policy on tardiness (e.g., no student is admitted into the classroom more than five minutes after class officially begins) and how you plan to handle those situations when they arise in the future. Also include specific language you can add to your course syllabus to address student tardiness.

Six Pro Tips for Being a Coach in the Classroom:

1) Correct Distracting Students

_____
_____
_____

2) Use Real-World Examples

_____
_____
_____

3) Show Genuine Interest in the Course Materials

_____
_____
_____

4) Demand Communication

_____
_____
_____

5) Encourage Students to Speak with Confidence

_____

_____

_____

6) Encourage Students to Think Big

_____

_____

_____

Chapter 5: Parent

He takes a personal interest in teaching the material, ensures students actually learn the material, and cares about and helps students discover concepts on their own.

—Anonymous student evaluation from Fall 2010

As stated in Chapter 1, the most important ingredient to being a successful and effective college instructor is to show that you genuinely care about your students and their success in the course. This ingredient is similar to the way a doting parent shows how much she cares for her own children. If you follow all of the other advice in this book but omit this ingredient, you will most likely be an unsuccessful instructor. It's just human nature that we'll put in more effort when we feel that someone we admire, whether it's our boss, partner, or college instructor, is genuinely invested in our success.

To show how much you truly care for your students, you should apply the following five tips:

1) Memorize each student's name.

2) Ask about students' hobbies and interests.

3) Include students' names in lectures and examples.

4) Contact absent students.

5) Praise students who read the assigned materials.

PRO TIP 1: Memorize Each Student's Name

As Dale Carnegie wisely noted in his famous book, *How to Win Friends and Influence People*, the sweetest sound to anyone is the sound of his own name. The most important thing you can do to connect with your students is to learn their names during the first class and often repeat their names thereafter. As Carnegie said, there is something magical about hearing your name spoken by someone else, especially in front of an audience.

On the first class of each semester, I begin by playing an icebreaker game as more fully explained in Chapter 7. Immediately afterward, I surprise the class by reciting the first name of each and every student without any help. Row by row, I call each student by name and watch their faces light up with a smile.

To do this, I apply four techniques: First, I learn at least one unique thing about each student during the icebreaker game and associate it with that student's name. For example, if Sheila mentions during the icebreaker game that she has nine cats, I might think of her as "Sheila the crazy cat lady." (Of course, I don't say that aloud for obvious reasons.) If Gabriel has visited 20 countries during his lifetime, I might think of him as "Gabriel the world traveler."

Second, I frequently repeat the names of my students out loud during the icebreaker game. For example, I might say, "So Gabriel, which country was your favorite?" or "Gabriel, please tell us more about your time in Japan."

Third, as I learn each student's name sitting in the front row, I will periodically stop for a moment to recite (silently in my head) the names of each person in that row before moving on to play the game with the second row.

Fourth, I usually point out any common connections be-tween two or more students during the icebreaker game. For example, if Jenny tells the class that she was born and raised in Japan before coming to the United States on a student visa, I might ask, "Gabriel, have you ever visited Jenny's home city of

Tokyo?" Consistent with the second technique above, I refer to both students by name as I ask them about their common connection. Finding a common connection between students will not only help you recall their names, it often establishes camaraderie between those particular students.

Once you have learned your students' names, it's important to call on each student by name at least once per class and continue that practice throughout the semester. After a few classes, your students will realize that you actually know everyone's first name by heart and they can expect to be called upon at least once during each class. This practice accomplishes two things: First, it puts your students on notice that they could be called upon to answer a question at any time (thus encouraging your students to stay alert and always come to class well prepared). Second, it shows that you care enough to learn their names. You would be amazed at how friendly and cooperative a classroom environment can be when everyone realizes that the instructor is on their side, is fully connected with each student, and honestly cares about their success. Unfortunately, the opposite is also quite true.

> **Fall 2008: He calls on people by name. He remembers everyone. He is excellent, and he is very inspiring. He really gives his all. He's great.**

> **Spring 2009: Mr. Kowis keeps the class engaged very well with good examples and student involvement.**

> **Fall 2014: Calls on us as students, asking questions and getting us involved with learning in the class discussion.**

> **Spring 2015: He calls on all students during class to give input on course material. This forces the class to stay engaged.**

PRO TIP 2: Ask about Students' Hobbies and Interests

Another way to connect with your students is to socialize with them before class and during breaks. The easiest way to do this is to simply ask them what they recently did for fun, what movies they saw, or whether they recently traveled anywhere interesting. I've found that most students are usually eager to share their thoughts or experiences. Shy students tend to be quiet when you pose general questions to the entire class, so you may have to ask them direct questions to get them to open up.

Socializing with your students may sound like a waste of time, but it's a great way to show that you genuinely care about them. Also, the more you get to know your students, the more comfortable they will feel asking or answering questions during class. Moreover, learning about your students' hobbies and interests will allow you to customize the examples or analogies that you use during class discussions so as to better pique their interest.

PRO TIP 3: Include Students' Names in Lectures and Examples

Many instructors use examples or analogies in class discussions to help explain a concept or set of rules that they're teaching. Whenever possible, you should use specific students in your class as characters in your examples. By adding one or two of your students to the example, you actively involve them and make things more interesting. Here is a typical exchange in my class:

> INSTRUCTOR: For purposes of this example, let's assume that Debbie (an actual student enrolled in your class) is talking to Jeff (another student enrolled in your class) in the parking lot about our last exam. Debbie's phone rings and she accidentally drops it. As she tries to catch her phone, she accidentally strikes Jeff in the face with the umbrella that she's holding. Jeff tried to duck, but he was too slow to avoid being hit by the umbrella. Debbie, do you think you just committed criminal assault, criminal battery, both, or neither crime?
>
> DEBBIE: I think neither crime because it was just an accident.
>
> INSTRUCTOR: Jeff, do you agree that neither crime was committed here? If so, why?
>
> JEFF: Yes, I think she is correct because both crimes require criminal intent and she didn't intend to hit me with her umbrella.
>
> INSTRUCTOR: You are both correct. Good job!

Just as most students love to hear the sound of their own name, they also enjoy seeing their name in print. So including your students' names on quizzes and tests is another effective way to grab their attention. This is especially effective if you can use their names in the context of a topic that they might be personally interested in. My students have often mentioned how much they enjoyed this.

Spring 2005: He involves everyone in the class, which in turn helps everyone learn from one another as well as the instructor.

Spring 2006: He is always happy and gets the class involved in the discussions so you also get to know the people in your class.

Fall 2008: He involves the class and he expects the best from you. I think that is admirable.

PRO TIP 4: Contact Absent Students

A few years ago, the college where I teach implemented a new policy encouraging us to contact absent students and advising them to either come back to class or consider withdrawing from the course before the drop date. The stated goal of this policy was to reduce the number of chronically absent students and thereby lower the number of students who ultimately fail the course. In my experience, it's not uncommon for at least one student each semester to suddenly stop attending class and never be seen on campus again. This situation usually leaves me in the awkward position of giving the missing student an "F" at the end of the semester. Although this new policy places some additional responsibility on me, it does result in fewer students failing the course, and my students usually appreciate a friendly phone call or email to check on them after a few unexplained absences. Bottom line, checking on your absent students shows that you genuinely care about them and their success in the course.

To be clear, I don't normally contact students after just one absence as that might be misinterpreted as harassment. The one exception here is that I might call or email a student after only one absence if a major exam will be given during the following class. Most students appreciate this reminder as it gives them a heads-up to prepare for the exam.

PRO TIP 5: Praise Students Who Read the Assigned Materials

One way to identify and acknowledge your students' dedication to the course is to ask for a show of hands at the beginning of each class to indicate whether they read the assigned chapters from the textbook. I usually praise those who raise their hands and challenge the other students to catch up on their reading before the next class. This approach achieves two important goals. First, it encourages students to come to class prepared. Second, it lets me know what level of participation to expect from my students during that class. If only a few students have read the assigned materials, you can expect them to pose fewer questions during the lecture and to give more incorrect responses to your questions.

Fall 2012: This is an easy class, but you have to read the book.

Checklist and Action Items

Select at least two Pro Tips from this chapter that you are willing to implement in your classroom. Under each tip that you select, write down specific details of how you plan to implement the tip. For example, perhaps you are planning to learn all of your students' names on the first day of class. Under the first tip below, write a brief description of what icebreaker game you can use to help you memorize everyone's names. Also include other ideas that might help you memorize their names, such as committing the class roster to memory a few days before the semester begins or creating a seating chart and bringing it with you to each class.

Five Pro Tips for Being a Parent in the Classroom:

1) Memorize Each Student's Name

_____

_____

_____

2) Ask about Students' Hobbies and Interests

_____

_____

_____

3) Include Students' Names in Lectures and Examples

_____

_____

_____

4) Contact Absent Students

_____

_____

_____

5) Praise Students Who Read the Assigned Materials

_____

_____

_____

PART III

Classroom Instruction

Chapter 6: Law Professor

He uses the Socratic Method, which prepares individuals for careers in business or if they are furthering their education in a field of law.

—Anonymous student evaluation from Fall 2013

College students should benefit from the Socratic Method, which is the teaching method most often employed by law professors to motivate their students to learn and develop critical thinking skills. The Socratic Method can be applied in almost any college classroom by presenting students with opposing viewpoints and then engaging in back-and-forth questioning until the students reach the correct answer.

The Socratic Method is an ancient form of teaching that was first introduced by the famous Greek philosopher Socrates. Rather than lecturing to his students, Socrates taught by engaging in a dialogue with his students that was based on the students' preexisting knowledge of a given topic. Through this dialogue (often called the "Socratic Dialogue"), Socrates would guide his students to the correct answer through a series of probing questions. The ultimate goal of this method is for students to exercise their logical and critical thinking skills to derive the correct answer.

The primary advantage of the Socratic Method is that it's more engaging than a traditional lecture. Instead of passively committing facts and concepts to rote memory and later regurgitating them on a test or other assignment, students are required to engage in a dialogue with either an instructor or another student while analyzing the strengths and weaknesses of differing viewpoints.

Traditionally, the Socratic Method entails asking open-ended questions involving general ideas with no right or wrong answers. For example, an instructor applying the Socratic

Method might ask her students for the best way to punish a convicted murderer. Obviously there are several different viewpoints on this topic and no one single answer is universally accepted as correct. The goal of such open-ended questioning is to begin a collaborative dialogue, either between the instructor and the student or between two or more students, that will lead to further analysis and eventually to a consensus of the correct or best answer. This dialogue is intended to be collaborative in that all parties are open to discovering the correct answer regardless of who may have presented that viewpoint first. The Socratic Method usually ends with either both parties being winners (reaching the correct conclusion) or both parties being losers (reaching the wrong conclusion).

The Socratic Method is much different than a traditional debate where each party sets forth a position on an issue and then attempts to persuade the other party that his own position is correct. A debate usually ends with a single winner and a single loser. The biggest difference between these two teaching methods is that only the Socratic Method requires students to apply logic and critical thinking skills to derive the correct answer. Accordingly, the Socratic Method should result in a deeper understanding of the assigned materials and concepts as compared to a traditional lecture.

At its most basic level, the Socratic Method of teaching involves the following two steps between the instructor and the student:

> Step 1: Students are assigned reading materials covering a particular topic, which they must read and analyze on their own before attending class. Without a general understanding of the assigned materials and concepts, the following dialogue would be fruitless.

> Step 2: The instructor engages a student in a dialogue about the topic. In this step, the instructor may present a hypothetical scenario and ask thought-provoking questions to discern whether the student fully understands the assigned materials and can reach the correct answer.

To initiate this dialogue, the instructor could cite the applicable rule of law and present a factual scenario. Next, the instructor could ask the student to apply the rule of law to the scenario and then derive the correct answer. It's also important to ask for the student's reasons that support her answer. If the student does not give the correct answer, the instructor can continue to question the student until she arrives at the correct answer and can support it with logical reasons. Oftentimes this may require redirecting the student to the applicable rule and asking her whether its requirements have been fully satisfied.

Alternatively, the instructor can apply the Socratic Method between two students as follows:

> Step 1: Students are assigned reading materials about a particular topic, which they must read and analyze on their own before attending class.

> Step 2: If all of the students in class do not initially agree on the correct answer to the hypothetical scenario posed by the instructor, the instructor may ask probing questions to two or more students who hold different viewpoints to see whether they can logically analyze the scenario and agree on the correct answer.

One way to initiate this discussion is to ask your students for a show of hands to find out who believes the answer to a particular question is X or Y. Then call on one student from each opposing position to give their best argument in support of their positions. With your guidance, allow both students the opportunity to fully explain their answers and give support for their answers until they both reach the correct answer.

In either approach, the overall goal of Socratic Dialogue is to make students evaluate their own positions and allow the dialogue to flow back and forth until the participants agree on the correct answer. If both participants agree as to the correct answer, then both participants have won. However, if an agreement on the correct answer is not reached by the end of the exercise or if both participants agree on an incorrect answer, then both participants have lost.

A simple example of the Socratic Dialogue from my class is as follows:

> INSTRUCTOR: Under common law, a criminal suspect may be able to avoid prosecution by raising the defense of duress. There are four requirements to qualify for the defense of duress, including the requirement that the harm threatened must be greater than the harm caused by the criminal suspect. In the following scenario, Stephen is accused of criminal assault and battery for an incident where Juan's arm was broken. Stephen admits to the attack on Juan, but places the blame on "One-Eyed" Jack, a hardened criminal and suspected leader of a local street gang. According to Stephen, Jack wanted to send a warning to Juan, the leader of a rival street gang. So Jack threatened to break Stephen's arm if Stephen didn't break Juan's arm as a warning. Can someone please tell me whether Stephen should be convicted of criminal assault and battery for his conduct?

> STUDENT: I think Stephen should not be convicted of criminal assault and battery.

> INSTRUCTOR: Why do you say that?

> STUDENT: I don't know. It just doesn't seem fair.

> INSTRUCTOR: Okay, but try to point to a specific rule of law that we discussed in class.

> STUDENT: Well, Stephen only broke Juan's arm after being threatened by that thug... Jack. So I think Stephen should be able to avoid conviction by claiming duress.

> INSTRUCTOR: Okay, so are you saying that all four requirements of the defense of duress were satisfied?

> STUDENT: Yes.

> INSTRUCTOR: Okay, please walk me through each of the four requirements so I can see how you reached your conclusion.

STUDENT: Oops. After reviewing the four requirements of duress, I now realize that one of the requirements is not satisfied. The harm threatened to Stephen was not greater than the harm that Stephen caused to Juan. I see now that Stephen won't be able to successfully raise the defense of duress and he will likely be convicted of criminal assault and battery in this set of facts.

INSTRUCTOR: That's correct! Good job.

In the above exchange, it was the student who ultimately realized the error and corrected his mistake. This back-and-forth process requires the student to actively engage in critical thinking and analysis, which is a key part of effective learning and much more powerful than merely listening to a traditional lecture.

As mentioned in the Preface, the Socratic Method of teaching is widely used in United States law schools as a way to motivate law students to read and analyze assigned cases. It's particularly effective for teaching first-year law students ("1Ls"), who are typically highly competitive and eager to display their intellectual prowess in front of their classmates. Although the Socratic Method is effective in the law school setting, it is also very intimidating as students are put on the spot and asked probing questions in front of the entire class. If a 1L selected for the Socratic Dialogue comes to class unprepared, the law professor will usually ridicule the student in front of the class in the same way that a harsh judge might embarrass an unprepared lawyer in the courtroom.

A typical law school Socratic Dialogue may occur as follows: Tenured and esteemed Professor Betty Johnson randomly calls on a 1L from her assigned seating chart. Her "victim" is Mr. Steve Dunkin, or "Flunkin Dunkin" as his classmates affectionately call him. Professor Johnson asks Steve to stand up and recite the relevant facts of the first assigned court case without looking at the textbook or his handwritten notes. After Steve sheepishly admits that he hasn't read the case yet, Professor Johnson calmly explains that her time is not to be wasted and asks Steve to immediately leave class for the day. As Steve, now red-faced with embarrassment, gathers his books and heads toward the door, Professor Johnson gives a stern warning to the entire class that ill-prepared attorneys and their clients may suffer a much worse fate if they show up in court unprepared.

Professor Johnson then randomly calls on another student, Ms. Yelena Smirnov, to stand and recite a brief summary of the facts for the first assigned case. If Yelena doesn't state all of the pertinent facts, the professor will usually ask for more details. If Yelena still can't recall all of the important facts, she may ask the professor for permission to refer to her textbook or hand-written notes for the purpose of refreshing her memory (not unlike a typical exchange between a judge and trial lawyer in a court of law). After Yelena refreshes her memory and recites the remaining facts, Professor Johnson then asks the student to state the key legal issue of the case.

If Yelena is unable to identify the legal issue, the professor will call on another student to give the correct legal issue. As stated above, most law students are übercompetitive and eager to correct their classmates in front of the entire class. Such students are often called "gunners" because they are quick to raise their hands and show that they know it all, or at least know more than their classmates. If the gunner is able to identify the correct legal issue for the case at hand, the original student is often ridiculed by the professor (sometimes in a joking manner and sometimes not) for failing to identify it. This exchange is unpleasant, but it results in a powerful lesson that the law student must always come to class prepared and be more careful when analyzing the case and legal issues.

As effective as the Socratic Method is for motivating law students, it may be too harsh for many undergraduate students. For that reason, you should use what I like to call the "Socratic-Lite" Method, as discussed in greater detail in the next section.

PRO TIP 1: Use the Socratic-Lite Method of Teaching

I have used the Socratic-Lite ("SL") Method with great success for the past 15 years and counting. The SL Method is largely based on the Socratic Method with certain adjustments to better suit undergraduate students. Specifically, the SL Method excludes excessively harsh ridicule and draconian consequences, like asking students to leave class if they arrived unprepared. Otherwise, the SL Method is very similar to the traditional Socratic Method. Under both methods, the instructor must ask her students probing questions and engage them in a Socratic Dialogue. This dialogue requires the instructor to openly challenge her students' answers and ask how they arrived at them. If a student gives an incorrect answer, the instructor could seek out another student who has a different answer and question both students until the correct answer is reached and understood by everyone.

There are several benefits to using the SL Method in college classes. First, it increases student engagement by challenging all students in the class, including shy students who normally don't volunteer to speak up or answer a question.

Second, the SL Method is an effective tool for monitoring how well the class understands the materials and allows the students to practice applying these materials to real-life situations. If you are covering a concept that has five required elements, you can ask a random student to apply those elements to a hypothetical situation and derive the correct outcome. Whether the student gives the correct answer or not, you should engage the student in Socratic Dialogue to make sure they completely understand the elements and how to reach the correct conclusion by applying those elements to the hypothetical situation. If this exercise fails and most students in the class don't seem to understand the materials or how to apply them, then you may need to spend more time explaining that particular concept and the elements related thereto.

Third, the SL Method also forces students to think critically about the topic and apply the set of rules/laws being discussed to arrive at the correct answer. If the student doesn't recall the set of rules/laws that apply to the particular question, then you should ask the student to find the applicable set of rules/laws in the assigned textbook and then answer the question. What you don't want to do is simply pass on this student and call on another student who already has the correct answer as that would completely avoid the purpose and benefits of applying the SL Method. If the student's first answer is incorrect, the SL Method requires the instructor to begin a Socratic Dialogue with the student to help her think through the situation until she finally reaches the correct answer. Alternatively, you can ask for different opinions from another student and then engage both students in a Socratic Dialogue until they jointly reach the correct answer.

Before we leave this topic, it's important to note that you are doing your shy students a great disservice if you avoid calling on them during class. I once had a shy student who requested that I refrain from calling on him in class. He said that he thoroughly enjoyed the first class of the semester and was looking forward to future classes, but he was concerned that he would feel uncomfortable if called upon to answer my questions in front of his classmates. To be clear, this was not a situation where the shy student suffered genuine anxiety from a documented mental condition or had a physical speech impairment.

I declined his request for a few reasons. First, the SL Method simply does not work without the Socratic Dialogue. Second, there is no way for the instructor to discover whether the shy student understands the materials if the instructor is not allowed to ask him challenging questions. Third, college instructors have a duty to prepare our students for their future careers, and allowing shy students to avoid answering questions will not prepare them for the verbal communication skills that most employers demand. You owe it to all of your students, including the shy ones, to challenge them to open up and answer questions in front of their peers. Furthermore, many of my students have told me at the end of the semester that the SL Method forced them to come out of their shell. These students will surely reap the benefits of overcoming their shyness as they interview for jobs and communicate with their supervisors, coworkers, and customers throughout their future careers.

> **Spring 2002: He is very concerned that the students understand his class. He encourages his students to participate in the class and asks them questions about the chapter. He makes his class very interesting and he evaluates us at the end of class.**

> **Fall 2002: I have not had a teacher that involves the students as much as Mr. Kowis.**

> **Fall 2006: He gives many examples and attempts to involve the class on a constant basis. He engages the class intellectually by providing background information supporting the logic of each topic's learning points, information that one would not discover in the text but only after extensive research.**

> **Spring 2006: After explaining the course material he will usually randomly call on someone to answer a question; this keeps your attention because he could call on you. Also, he writes everything on the board so that I can take very detailed notes.**

> **Spring 2008: I'm particularly interested in this subject, but it could have become a boring class with the wrong instructor. I very much enjoyed his lectures. He gives great examples to help explain the legal issues that we're discussing. As much as I hate to be called on in class, it makes me come prepared (and has made it easier to make good grades).**

> **Fall 2009: Mr. Kowis is very interactive with the class, he keeps you engaged.**

> **Fall 2010: Involves us in class whether we choose to or not. He gives great real-life examples of what he his teaching to the class.**

Fall 2012: Professor Kowis actively engages the class. It is not a mere lecture class and it keeps everyone involved and awake. His teaching style is refreshing and after not being in school for a while, it was welcomed.

Checklist and Action Items

If you have never utilized the SL Method in your classroom, think of at least three lecture topics for your next course that you could teach with this method. Under each lecture topic below, write down specific details of how you plan to implement the SL Method. For example, perhaps you are planning to give a lesson in your next Political Science course regarding the recent Supreme Court decision in *United States v. Texas*, 195 L. Ed. 2d 638 (2016) and whether this court was correct to affirm a preliminary injunction to temporarily block President Obama's controversial immigration program. For this lesson, you could develop a short list of questions to pose to two students with opposing viewpoints on this case and thereby engage them in Socratic Dialogue regarding this topic.

Lecture Topic 1:

_____
_____
_____

Lecture Topic 2:

_____
_____
_____

Lecture Topic 3:

_____
_____
_____

Chapter 7: Classroom Teacher

Mr. Kowis engages each and every student throughout the entire semester. He takes the time at the beginning of the semester to learn each student's name and a little about them. I believe this is a very effective tool to gain the students' respect and engage the students the entire semester.

—Anonymous student evaluation from Fall 2013

Obviously, you can't be an effective college instructor without being an effective classroom teacher. In other words, you must have good classroom management skills and be able to effectively communicate lessons to your students. After all, classroom teaching is much more than merely standing at the dry erase board and reading verbatim from a textbook. To hone your classroom teacher skills, you should apply the following nine tips:

1) Start the semester with a fun icebreaker game.
2) Never hide the ball.
3) Give bonus points for the course evaluation.
4) Give candy bribes to encourage attendance.
5) Give an easy daily quiz at the end of each class to reinforce materials.
6) Use peer grading for daily assignments and quizzes.
7) Give interesting exams with a mixture of question types.
8) Review graded exams in class.
9) Advise students to pre-read and attend all classes.

PRO TIP 1: Start the Semester with a Fun Icebreaker Game

Icebreaker games are a popular way to kick off the beginning of a semester and help students get to know one another as well as their instructor. The best icebreaker games are entertaining and draw your students closer to one another by getting them talking about common or unique interests. My favorite is a game that I like to call "Two Truths and One Lie." This icebreaker not only helps students get to know one another, it also forces them to get used to speaking in front of the class. Just as important, it will help you learn your students' names, which is easier once you've learned something interesting and unique about each one, as I discussed in Chapter 5.

This icebreaker game is simple. The instructor calls on one student at a time, who must give three statements about herself. These three statements can be anything that describes the student or her personal interests, but the one requirement is she must include two true statements and one lie (which the student should list in any order she chooses). The instructor writes all three statements on the whiteboard and then asks the rest of the class to vote by show of hands for the statement they believe is a lie. After everyone votes, the student who gave the three statements reveals which statement is the lie.

The three statements can be anything that students want to share about themselves. These statements usually involve general topics such as the number of kids, grandkids, or pets they have, the number of years they have been married, the number of countries they've visited, the places they were born, and their current day job or college major. Sometimes the students' statements include more personal topics such as their favorite hobbies, foods, or music, or their future career plans. The more unique the three statements are, the more challenging it will be to identify the lie. More important, knowing something unique about each student (e.g., Brittany got arrested during a first date as the result of 13 unpaid parking tickets or Wes has an embarrassing tattoo of Justin Bieber that he got while celebrating his 21st birthday in Las Vegas) will make it easier for you to memorize their names.

Before my students begin this icebreaker game, I demonstrate how the game is played by giving the class three statements about myself and then asking the class to guess the lie. For example, here are the three statements that I recently gave:

1) I am a two-time Olympian who competed in the Men's Individual Archery competitions during the 1996 Atlanta Games and the 2000 Sydney Games. I did not earn a medal in either event, but it was an honor to represent my country.

2) I have earned three academic degrees at the bachelor's level and above.

3) My favorite hobby is racing off-road vehicles (aka "four-wheelers").

I asked the class to raise their hands if they thought I was lying about statement number one. Then I repeated this same question for statements two and three. When the votes were tallied, approximately 15% of the class thought I was lying about being a two-time Olympian, 25% thought I was lying about earning three academic degrees, and the majority (60%) thought I was lying about racing four-wheelers as a personal hobby. Much to the students' surprise, I was lying about being an Olympian.

Over the years, my students have made some interesting statements while playing this icebreaker game. Once, a male student in his late 30s or early 40s told the class that he was a minister in a church. Because of his tidy appearance and respectable demeanor, the class was very surprised to learn that this was his untrue statement. "Who lies about being a church minister?" I asked. "I'm pretty sure the Bible says you'll go straight to hell for that!" The class erupted in laughter.

Another interesting statement came from a student who was taking the class with his lovely wife. He professed to the entire class with a straight face that he was a famous porn star. This statement was an obvious lie given his portly physique and marital status. As soon as he made this ludicrous statement, the room filled with smiles and awkward laughter, and I couldn't decide whether I was more embarrassed for him or his poor embarrassed wife sitting right next to him.

PRO TIP 2: Never Hide the Ball

One of the key goals of every good college instructor is to create an atmosphere where your students are successful. To do that, it is imperative that you precisely spell out what you expect from your students on all upcoming assignments and exams. If your students must memorize and be able to describe all 118 elements of the periodic table for the first exam, then you should expressly tell them that.

In law school, professors are notorious for hiding the ball. In other words, they don't give a traditional lecture regarding the information that they want their students to learn. They also don't give direct answers to the questions that their students ask. As described in Chapter 6, they usually assign certain cases in the textbook and ask their students to be prepared to discuss those cases. During class, the law professor will randomly select one student to stand up and summarize one or more of the assigned cases. As the law student discusses the case, the law professor usually interjects with probing questions (i.e., Socratic Dialogue) to help the student think critically about the case and better understand how the judge applied the applicable law to the facts and reached the decision.

Unlike traditional lectures, the Socratic Method places the primary responsibility on the law student to analyze the assigned cases. In fact, the law professor does not present the key information directly to students—hence, the law professor is said to be "hiding the ball," and it's up to the students to find it. The bottom line is that this intense process works well in law school, but it's usually not appropriate for an undergraduate classroom. Instead, you should present the relevant information and directly explain it to your students.

For example, I often give my students one short list of elements or criteria that they are expected to memorize and understand before the next major exam. Then I follow up by asking a random student to recite this list any time the topic arises in class. By tipping off my students that this particular list of elements is important and will definitely be on the next major exam, I encourage them to study those elements.

To illustrate, I usually give my students a list of the four elements for negligence, which includes duty of care, breach of duty, causation, and damages.[7] To help students memorize this list, I usually refer to the 2011 chick-flick *Something Borrowed,* wherein a law student named Rachel memorizes the same list of elements using the mnemonic "Don't Blame Cameron Diaz." This clever trick usually helps my students recall these four elements. More important, they are much more likely to learn these elements if they are expressly told that they are expected to know them for the upcoming exam.

Fall 2002: Explains exactly what we need to learn.

Spring 2006: He writes what is important on the board, so not only do we hear what he's saying, but we see it as well.

Fall 2007: He encourages participation and is very clear about student expectations.

---

[7] You can see an example test question covering the four elements of negligence in Pro Tip 7 of this chapter.

PRO TIP 3: Give Bonus Points for the Course Evaluation

One popular tool for measuring the effectiveness of a college instructor's teaching style and identifying areas for improvement is the anonymous course evaluation that students may complete near the end of each semester. At the college where I teach, students' course evaluations are usually available online or handed out to students in paper form during the last month of each semester. I usually take my students' course evaluations to heart, but with a grain of salt as well. In other words, it is typical for at least one student in every class to report that she absolutely loved how I taught the course and at least one student to report that he completely abhorred my teaching style no matter how well I actually performed. I usually ignore those few outliers as somehow biased or inaccurate.

What should really concern you is the opinion of the remaining body of students, whose makeup is typically 90% or more of the total class. If these folks were generally happy with your teaching style and how much they learned from the class, you should consider the semester to have been a success. On the other hand, if more than a few of those students from the 90% were unhappy with the class or pointed to a common problem they perceived, you should take a hard look at those problems and decide whether changes are warranted.

At most colleges, student course evaluations are completely voluntary. To encourage my students to complete the course evaluation, I offer a few bonus points to be added to their quiz average. (To keep my students' evaluations anonymous, I only ask my students to turn in the sheet of paper that indicates they completed the online course evaluation for my class. For semesters when the college administers a paper evaluation at the beginning of a particular class, I usually step out of the classroom until they have finished the evaluations and take a roll call immediately afterward to give credit for those students who participated in the paper survey.)

This incentive works well, and I typically have an 80% or higher participation rate from my students. I believe that giving a few bonus points is a small price to pay for the ability to see how my students perceive my teaching style and to pinpoint any problem areas that might exist.

PRO TIP 4: Give Candy Bribes to Encourage Attendance

Like many instructors, I typically give a brief (say, ten-minute) review during the class immediately preceding the test. However, I give a more thorough review for the final exam. In fact, I devote an entire three-hour class to prepare my students for their cumulative final exam.

To boost the attendance of this important review session, I announce that I will be handing out candy. However, I don't do this at random. Instead, I ask each student a review question and distribute candy only to those who give the correct answer. If they get it wrong, I usually bark "No candy for you!" in my best "Soup Nazi" voice. But I typically ask each student multiple questions during this three-hour review session, so everyone has plenty of chances to satisfy their sweet tooth.

For obvious reasons, this review session is usually the most fun class of the semester. It is filled with corny jokes and big smiles as everyone enjoys their favorite candy while I cover the review materials at a relaxed pace. I also find this class to be personally rewarding because I can gauge how much knowledge my students have acquired from their 16-week course.

Instead of distributing candy, you could bring pizza or donuts for the entire class to enjoy during the review. However, I find that trading candy for correct answers works best as it shows a direct correlation between knowing the right answer and receiving an "award" for it. If your students can freely help themselves to all the pizza or donuts they want, there is no such correlation and they are more likely to zone out during the review session soon after the "sugar rush" or leave at the mid-class break.

Spring 2013: Kowis is the absolute best professor I have had. He is professional, respectful, and FUN! Learning was easy, and I looked forward to his class every single day. And he is bringing us candy. Who does that anymore? AWESOME PROF.

PRO TIP 5: Give an Easy Daily Quiz at the End of Each Class to Reinforce Materials

Before I taught my very first college class, I put a lot of thought into how I could encourage students to attend class and also keep them in their seats until the final bell rang. Those are not the easiest goals for a typical college student who tends to have the mindset of "the instructor has her schedule and I have mine." The solution that I came up with was to give an easy quiz at the end of each class.

These quizzes should result in an effortless "A" for everyone who bothers to show up for class and pay attention during the lecture. In fact, my students usually don't have to read the assigned chapters to get an excellent score on their daily quizzes.[8] To make these quizzes straightforward, I often spoon-feed the class the exact materials that will be on the quiz. For example, I frequently drop obvious hints as I give my lecture by saying something like "hint, hint, wink, wink, be sure to take good notes here." That little phrase typically brings my students' pencils or typing fingers to quick attention.

Giving an easy daily quiz provides four benefits to my students. First, it encourages them to attend every class because they know their quiz average will be significantly reduced by any absences. Second, it encourages them to pay attention because they know they will be quizzed on the materials covered in the lecture. Third, it encourages them to stay in class throughout the entire class period so they can take the quiz. (In a three-hour night class, many college students tend to disappear at the mid-class break unless the instructor gives an incentive to stay.) Fourth, they can use their graded quizzes as study aids for their upcoming exams.

Based on the course evaluations that I've received over the years, my students usually view these daily quizzes in a positive light rather than as a punishment. This is because each quiz is

---

[8] However, the same cannot be said about my exams. If my students don't read the assigned chapters, their test scores will usually suffer.

brief (usually ten or 12 questions) and is designed to be an "easy A" as explained above. In fact, most of my students earn an "A" or "B" on their daily quizzes (even if they didn't bother to read the assigned chapters ahead of time), which helps boost their overall grade in the course. In other words, the quizzes are designed to be a reward for coming to class and paying attention.

Here is an example of a typical daily quiz that I use in my Business Law class:

Business Law Quiz Three

NAME: _____

TRUE OR FALSE:

(Write the *entire word* "TRUE" or "FALSE" in the answer space.)

1) _____ The law consists of enforceable rules governing relationships among individuals and between individuals and their society.

2) _____ *Stare decisis* refers to the practice of deciding new cases based on past decisions involving similar legal issues and facts.

3) _____ Statutes are a secondary source of law.

4) _____ The Uniform Commercial Code (UCC) is a federal law that was enacted by Congress.

5) _____ In most American states today, the same courts can grant both legal and equitable remedies.

6) _____ A defendant is a party that files a lawsuit.

MATCHING:

(Write *only* the letter of your answer choice in the answer space.)

      A. jurisprudence   E. England

      B. France   F. Texas

C. Louisiana   G. precedent

D. Mexico   H. legal realism

7) _____ Name of place that the United States bases most of its legal system from.

8) _____ Name of place that only adopted half of UCC and has a mixed legal system of Common Law and Civil Law.

9) _____ This word refers to a previously decided case that is recognized as authority for deciding future cases involving similar legal issues and facts.

MULTIPLE CHOICE:

(Write *only* the letter of your answer choice in the answer space.)

10) _____ Kim and Khloé are discussing various legal philosophies. Which of the following statements made by Khloé is FALSE?

> A. According to the Natural Law philosophy, the law should reflect universal moral and ethical principles that are part of human nature.
>
> B. Legal Positivists believe that there can be no higher law than a nation's written law.
>
> C. Legal Realists believe that the law should be applied the same in all cases regardless of the particular circumstances involved.
>
> D. According to the Historical philosophy, emphasis is placed on the origin and history of each law.

11) _____ George Strait files a lawsuit against Eminem alleging that Eminem reproduced one of George's songs without his permission. In deciding this case, a U.S. court must apply the doctrine of *stare decisis*. This doctrine has several benefits, including:

> A. Greater predictability
>
> B. Greater stability

C. Greater stability and greater predictability

D. None of the above

12) _____ Which of the following is a TRUE statement about the distinction between Courts of Law and Courts of Equity?

A. Today, most US states maintain separate Courts of Law and Courts of Equity.

B. Money damages may be awarded in both a Court of Equity and a Court of Law.

C. Courts of Equity involve different remedies from those available in Courts of Law.

D. None of the above is true.

13) _____ Statutory Law of the US includes:

A. The statutes and ordinances enacted by Congress, state legislatures, and local governments

B. The law established by Courts of Equity

C. The law established by Courts of Law

D. All of the above

14) _____ Common Law is a legal system that places emphasis on:

A. Legislation

B. Statutory code

C. Case law

D. Principles of Equity

EXTRA CREDIT:

Name the four parts of the IRAC legal reasoning and analysis process.[9]

1) I _____

2) R _____

3) A _____

4) C _____

> **Fall 2002: Mr. Kowis gives us quizzes after each class session. It helps us remember what he was teaching that day.**

> **Fall 2010: The instructor asks each student questions on the subject matter each class, plus there is a quiz at the end of every class to make sure we retain the materials.**

> **Fall 2012: I also love the quiz at the end of each class. It's very helpful to refresh our memory right then and later.**

> **Spring 2013: He goes over what we need to understand and by having the quizzes every single class day. As much as I hate the quizzes, it does allow me to understand better.**

> **Fall 2013: I also liked that he gives a quiz every week. It seemed like a tough policy at first, but it helped me tremendously in disciplining myself and learning the material.**

> **Fall 2014: He lectures in a way that makes taking notes very easy, and he gives a short quiz after each lecture which helps the students memorize the material and study for the tests.**

---

[9] For those of you playing at home, the correct answers are: 1) True, 2) True, 3) False, 4) False, 5) True, 6) False, 7) E, 8) C, 9) G, 10) C, 11) C, 12) C, 13) A, 14), C; and Issue, Rule of Law, Application of Law to the Facts, and Conclusion for the extra credit.

Spring 2016: I know I hate the quiz he gives at the end of class, but it makes you pay attention because you know you will be quizzed after the lecture.

PRO TIP 6: Use Peer Grading for Daily Quizzes and Assignments

To help students better understand the materials covered on each quiz, you should instruct them to exchange their quizzes with each other and grade them in class as you call out the correct answers. After your students grade each other's quizzes and return them to their rightful owners, you can collect the graded quizzes so you can record them in your gradebook and then pass them out at the next class. To speed up this process, I recommend that you ask your students to come forward one at a time to show you their graded quiz. This process will allow you to record all quiz grades immediately and allow your students to keep their graded quizzes for review and study purposes.

Peer grading the quizzes provides three benefits to my students. First, it gives students a second chance to review the questions and answers immediately after they take the quiz. Second, it allows my students to ask me about any particular questions or answers that confused them. Third, my students get instant feedback instead of having to wait until the following class.[10]

Obviously, peer grading also provides you with a significant benefit too. Rather than taking your time to collect the daily quizzes, grade them, record the grades and distribute them to your students during the next class, you can use that saved time for other important duties. You're welcome!

---

[10] The peer grading process has been blessed by the U.S. Supreme Court as a valuable teaching tool that does not violate the Family Educational Rights and Privacy Act of 1974. See *Owasso Ind. School District v. Falvo*, 534 U.S. 426 (2002).

PRO TIP 7: Give Interesting Exams with a Mixture of Question Types

Let's face it, tests are a necessary evil in college. Although they are stressful for your students and time-consuming for you, there's no better way to evaluate a student's mastery of the knowledge and skills required by the course. Fortunately, there are many ways to design a test for your students. College tests typically consist of long essays, short-answer essays, multiple choice, matching, fill-in-the-blank, true/false questions, and hands-on tasks (e.g., science lab work). I strive to create tests utilizing as many of those different question types as possible so as to provide a fair chance of success to all students. If you design a test with a single type of test question (e.g., long essays), you could be giving an undue advantage to students who excel in that format over those who struggle with it.

Tests with a variety of question types are very common for many state examinations. For example, when I took the three-day Texas bar exam (for prospective lawyers) a few decades ago, it contained a combination of multiple-choice questions, long essays, and fill-in-the-blank questions. Similarly, the Uniform Certified Public Accountant Examination (for prospective CPAs) contains a combination of multiple-choice questions and condensed case studies. The United States Medical Licensure Exam (for prospective physicians) contains a combination of multiple-choice questions, simulated patient interactions, and clinical case simulations.

Here are excerpts from a typical test that I might use in my Business Law course, which as you can see, employ a wide variety of question types.

Business Law Test One

NAME: _____

TRUE OR FALSE:

(Write the *entire word* "TRUE" or "FALSE" in the answer space.

NOTE: * PLEASE WRITE NEATLY *****

If I can't read your answer, I will mark it incorrect!)

_____ 1. A long arm statute is a state law that permits state courts to obtain personal jurisdiction over nonresident defendants.

MULTIPLE CHOICE:

(*Fill in the blank* with the letter choice that best completes the statement or best answers the question. *NOTE: Circled letter choices will be ignored!!*)

_____ 22. Cody is a life-long resident of Texas. While driving through New Orleans, Louisiana, while on vacation, Cody accidentally runs over Victoria as she walks along a crowded sidewalk. Victoria is a life-long resident of Louisiana. Cody does not own property in Louisiana and has never visited Louisiana before this trip. Victoria files a lawsuit against Cody in Louisiana state court to recover the cost of her medical bills due to this accident. Regarding Cody, the Louisiana state court:

    A. can exercise diversity jurisdiction.

    B. can exercise *in rem* jurisdiction.

    C. can exercise *in personam* jurisdiction.

    D. cannot exercise jurisdiction.

SHORT ANSWER ESSAY:

(Write a few sentences to answer the following questions. NOTE: I will **NOT** read more than a few sentences, <u>**so please *be brief* and *write neatly*!!**</u>).

44. In one to three brief sentences, define the doctrine of *stare decisis*.

_____

_____

_____

_____

FILL IN THE BLANK:

(Write the correct answer in the blank space below.)

***HINT: The correct answers come from the chapter on Genuineness of Assent.

51. Johnson, Inc., which owns many furniture stores nationwide, opens a new store in a small town made up of mostly poor and uneducated citizens. Because Johnson's new store is the only furniture store located within 1,000 miles of this town, its citizens have no other options for buying furniture. With the sole purpose of being greedy, Johnson prices its furniture 50 times higher than the typical retail prices listed at its other stores. With little or no bargaining power and no other alternatives, many citizens of this town sign commercially unreasonable contracts with Johnson to buy furniture. These contracts contain one-sided terms that are so grossly unfair as to be "void of conscience." This contract is called an _____ contract. (1 word)

MATCHING:

(Fill in the blank below with the correct letter choice.)

A. Reformation	D. Delegation of Duties
B. Release	E. Rescission
C. Promissory Estoppel	F. Anticipatory Repudiation

_____ 63. The unmaking of a contract so as to return the parties to the positions they held before the contract was made.

EXTRA CREDIT QUESTIONS:

(Write the correct answers in the blank spaces below.)

1) List the four elements of negligence:

    a) _____

    b) _____

    c) _____

    d) _____

You should always include clear instructions for each type of test question. For example, I require my students to spell out the entire word "True" or "False" in the answer blanks for true/false questions because many college students have poor handwriting. A sloppy "T" can be indistinguishable from a sloppy "F." If I can't read the sloppy answer, I will mark it incorrect per the instructions boldly stated on the test.

As another example, I require my students to write the correct answer in the appropriate blank space for multiple-choice questions rather than simply circle the letter choice. I require this because students often circle more than one letter choice as they puzzle over the answer choices and then forget to scratch out or erase the unintended circles. Also, I can grade multiple-choice questions much more quickly when the answers are written in the answer blanks lined up on the left side of the page. If a student forgets to write the answer in the answer blanks, I try to decipher which answer choice the student intended to choose by looking at the circled answers. If the student circled more than one answer and it's unclear which answer was intended, I will mark it incorrect.

Each style of test question has its own pros and cons, and some are better suited for evaluating certain skill sets than others. For example, matching and fill-in-the-blank questions are excellent for testing vocabulary. Essay questions are an excellent gauge of whether students can correctly identify legal issues. As far as cons, many students find true/false questions to be tricky. For that reason, I make these questions as unambiguous as possible. For example, when testing students on the three types of statutory laws (Federal, state, and local), I might word the true/false question as "There are only two types of statutory laws, which are Federal and state laws)." In this sentence, the qualifier "only" and the two listed types of laws make it crystal clear that the sentence can only be true if there are in fact only two types of statutory laws. If the student incorrectly answers "True," it will be because the student failed to recognize the third type of statutory laws (local laws). This approach would be preferable to a vague true/false question such as "Statute law includes Federal and state laws." This may or may not be true depending on how you read it.

I recommend giving at least a few extra credit questions on each test. The reason for this is twofold. First, in the event that a student complains that a test question is poorly written or unnecessarily tricky, you can point to the chance to earn extra credit points as a remedy for this potentially unfair situation. In the rare cases when my students have raised this complaint about my test questions, this answer has always seemed to appease them. Second, the extra credit section provides a good opportunity to ask tougher questions, which challenges the brightest students and keeps them from growing bored.

To make your test questions more interesting, you should do the following three things:

1) Include the first names of your students in the questions. This tip only takes a few extra minutes, and it creates additional interest in the exam. At some point most students will start to notice that their classmates' names are included on the test and will anticipate eventually seeing their own name on the test too.

2) Include the names of famous celebrities and TV show characters in the test questions. Students will also find this more interesting than using John or Jane Doe in all questions. For example, I've occasionally refer-

enced characters from the wildly popular *Simpsons* TV show in my test questions, as follows:

_____ 23. Without having probable cause, Police Chief Wiggum suspects that Homer was involved in a recent aggravated robbery of Apu's convenience store. After conducting an illegal search of Homer's car, Wiggum finds a knife that he believes was used in the crime. Wiggum immediately arrests and charges Homer for the robbery. At Homer's trial, the knife will most likely be:

A. Admitted as evidence of Homer's crime.

B. Admitted only as proof of Homer's guilty state of mind.

C. Admitted as proof of Police Chief Wiggum's suspicions.

D. Excluded from the evidence presented in court.

3) Include silly or ridiculous scenarios in the test questions. Doing this often provokes random laughter from my students during an otherwise boring exam period. For example, the following questions have put a smile on the faces of at least a few of my students:

_____ 12. Dudley and Bonkers agree to create a new business together with the purpose of making money by washing donkeys at local petting zoos. They agree to equally share the profits, losses, and management rights as co-owners of the business. They do not formally declare that their donkey-washing business has a specific form of organization. Dudley and Bonker's business is a:

A. Sole proprietorship.

B. General partnership.

C. Corporation.

D. None of the above.

_____ 31. At a local crack house, "Buffalo" Bill buys some illegal drugs from "Sweet Roll" Tiffany. Because Mr. Bill believes that Ms. Tiffany overcharged him for this purchase, Mr. Bill purposely shoves Ms. Tiffany to the ground. Although Ms. Tiffany was not physically injured from the shove, she sues Mr. Bill in civil court alleging that the shove was a battery. Mr. Bill is liable for the tort of battery only if:

A. Ms. Tiffany was afraid of Mr. Bill.

B. The shove was harmful or offensive to an ordinary reasonably prudent person.

C. Mr. Bill was not overcharged for his drugs.

D. Mr. Bill acted with malice and an evil motive toward Ms. Tiffany.

PRO TIP 8: Review Graded Exams in Class

You should always grade major exams outside of the classroom and return them at the beginning of the following class period. In that next class, you should review the answers to the exam and take questions from students if they are confused. I allow my students to keep their graded exams for use as a study aid for their cumulative final exam.

Reviewing the graded exam in class accomplishes three things: First, it helps students understand why their answers were marked right or wrong. Second, it allows each student to ask you about anything that causes concern or needs clarification. Third, it helps students retain the materials covered on the exam while it is still fresh on their minds.

PRO TIP 9: Advise Students to Pre-Read and Attend All Classes

If you only take away one tip from this book, make sure that it's this one. Having spent eight years as a full-time student in college and law school plus another 15 years teaching as a college instructor, I have consistently observed two common habits of "A" students: excellent class attendance and consistently reading the assigned materials before coming to class. Students who make it a habit of skipping classes or ignoring the assigned readings tend to earn mediocre grades at best.

To help my students succeed in my class (and give them the skills to succeed in their other classes as well), I reinforce the above two habits with my students every time I return their graded exams (excluding the final exam, of course). Specifically, I ask the handful of students who scored the highest on the exam to stand in recognition of their achievement. Then I ask those students to raise their hands if they attended every class leading up to the most-recent exam and then again if they typically read the assigned chapters before coming to each class. Having done this exercise for 15 years, I have consistently observed that at least 90% of my top-scoring students raise their hands for perfect class attendance and at least 85% indicate they often read the assigned chapters before class. Then I usually caution my students that these two steps are not a magic pill and won't guarantee an "A" in any particular course. However, they should greatly increase the chances of excelling in my course and any other college courses that they take.

Another way to encourage your students to read is by asking for a show of hands from the students who read the assigned chapters. I do this at the beginning of each and every class, excluding days where I administer an exam. About three or four weeks into the semester, the number of hands indicating that they have read the chapters usually goes down, sometimes significantly. When that happens, I will sometimes select a random student to write the following quote on the board:

"A person who won't read has no advantage over one who can't read."

—Mark Twain

I'm not trying to shame students who don't read. Rather, I want them to understand that college is an opportunity to grow and improve oneself. Simply put, growth won't happen if the student refuses to do the work.

> **Fall 2013: He was right. Keeping up with reading before class helped me keep up/understand the material and learn even more in class.**

Checklist and Action Items

Select at least three Pro Tips from this chapter that you are willing to implement in your classroom. Under each tip that you select, write down specific details of how you plan to implement the tip. For example, perhaps you are planning to use a fun icebreaker game on the first day of class. Under the first tip below, write a brief description of a few icebreaker games that you might want to try in your classroom and then write the pros and cons for each game to see which one works best for you. Alternatively, you could try different icebreaker games for different semesters and then decide which one you like best.

Nine Pro Tips for Being an Effective Classroom Teacher:

1) Start the Semester with a Fun Icebreaker Game

_____

_____

_____

2) Never Hide the Ball

_____

_____

_____

3) Give Bonus Points for the Course Evaluation

_____

_____

_____

4) Give Candy Bribes to Encourage Attendance

_____

_____

_____

5) Give an Easy Daily Quiz at the End of Each Class to Reinforce Materials

_____
_____
_____

6) Use Peer Grading for Daily Assignments and Quizzes

_____
_____
_____

7) Give Interesting Exams with a Mixture of Question Types

_____
_____
_____

8) Review Graded Exams in Class

_____
_____
_____

9) Advise Students to Pre-Read and Attend All Classes

_____
_____
_____

PART IV

Planning a Great Class

Chapter 8: A Roadmap to Success

He outlines very clearly the material that you need to learn and the reasons it is important.

—Anonymous student evaluation from Fall 2009

A mountain climber does not reach the top of Mount Everest without first making careful preparations for the treacherous journey ahead. Similarly, a college instructor must carefully plan for the upcoming semester. To prepare for a successful course, you should apply the following five tips:

1) Create a concise syllabus and course calendar.

2) Structure the syllabus around the textbook.

3) Be firm but fair.

4) Be flexible when needed and revise future Syllabi.

5) Remind students of semester progress.

PRO TIP 1: Create a Concise Syllabus and Course Calendar

When I was in college in the late '80s and early '90s, the typical course syllabus was a one-page document that contained nothing more than the key ingredients. A lot has changed over the past quarter-century and today's typical course syllabus (like the American waistline) has grown by leaps and bounds.

The college where I teach requires its instructors to use a course syllabus filled with multiple pages of superfluous information, or "fluff" as I like to call it. Fluff includes any and all information that can be easily found in the college's student catalog or on their website, such as school policies on equal opportunities for all students, student rights under the Americans with Disabilities Act of 1990, recommendations for computer virus protection, and academic integrity standards. Fluff also includes the college's standard policies on required or recommended course prerequisites to register for the course, the number of credit hours awarded for successful completion of the course, expected learning outcomes for the course, course withdrawal deadlines, tuition refunds, classroom behavior requirements, general information on available degree plans, and contact information for the various deans and chairpersons.

Granted, these topics may occasionally become relevant for a few students. However, the vast majority of students have no interest in general policies unless and until they are accused of violating these policies or the general policy becomes relevant for their particular situation. In any case, the few students who are interested in this information can easily find it, and in greater detail, in the college's course catalogue or on its website. More important, adding this unnecessary information only makes the syllabus longer and students tend to ignore the entire thing if it's too long. For these reasons, the ideal course syllabus should not include any fluff.

If fluff is required by the college where you teach, you should place the fluff in the middle of the syllabus (if allowed by the college) where the reader's attention level is typically at its lowest point. For example, you could place the instructor's contact information, the required textbook, specific grading policies, and the like on the front page and the detailed course calendar on the last page. If students choose to peruse the fluff in the middle pages, that is their choice.

The ideal course syllabus should explain how the instructor intends to run the course and establish clear expectations for the student. The key is to provide sufficient information to inform the students of what is expected from them throughout the semester. In addition to providing your vital contact information and office hours, the syllabus must also set forth a road map of the materials to be covered during the entire course and establish concrete deadlines for each assignment. If designed properly, a course syllabus should help avoid common problems that could otherwise occur. In fact, college administrators often advise that most student complaints can be avoided simply by specifically addressing potential problems in the syllabus. For example, if a student complains to the dean that the instructor refused to accept a late assignment, the first thing the dean will ask is whether late assignments are covered in the syllabus. If your syllabus does cover this topic and the stated penalty is plainly spelled out, the student's complaint will most likely be immediately dismissed. If your syllabus does not address this topic or if it does so in a vague fashion, the dean is more likely to side with the student and override your penalty.

Ideally, a course syllabus should be brief (a few pages or less if your college allows it) and focused on the following key ingredients:

1) The instructor's name, contact information, and available office hours,

2) The required textbook and other materials,

3) Policies on grading,

4) Policies on absenteeism, tardiness, and make-up tests,

5) Policies on common problems, including specific penalties for late assignments, unauthorized cellphone usage during class, and where to seek information in the event of school closings for bad weather, and

6) A detailed course calendar that includes assigned readings for each class and due dates for all assignments, quizzes, and tests.

In a typical 16-week college course, students are usually expected to read and understand hundreds of pages from an assigned textbook or other publication that covers a wide variety of topics in great detail. With so much material to cover in such a short time frame, it is easy to understand why many college students feel overwhelmed and lost. The first thing you can do to help alleviate their anxieties and help them understand how a particular topic fits into the overall course materials is to provide the class with a calendar or schedule that lays out exactly which chapters and materials will be covered in each class and when the tests, quizzes, and other assignments are due. This course calendar is usually provided as part of the syllabus and handed out on the first day of class.

Spring 2006: The syllabus was exact.

Here is an example of an ideal syllabus,[11] including a detailed course calendar:

---

[11] NOTE: the following syllabus would print on only two pages if you use single line spacing.

Kowis State College

(Home of the Fighting Llamas)

Course Syllabus

Course Title/No: Business Law 101 / BUSL 101.1234

Course Description: An introductory course that covers common law regarding various business activities such as contracts, torts, criminal law, choice of business entities, strict product liability, and intellectual property rights

Semester: Fall 2020

Instructor: Mike Kowis, J.D., LL.M.

Contact Info: (123) 456-7890/ mikekowis@kowisstatecollege.edu

Office Hours: 9 p.m. to 9:30 p.m., Tuesdays & other times by appointment

Textbook: Kowis, *American Business Law at Its Finest* (3rd edition)

Grades: There will be four major grades totaling 400 points as follows:

Exam 1:	100 points
Exam 2:	100 points
Final Exam:	100 points
Quiz Avg. (includes bonus points):	100 points

Final letter grades for this course will be assigned as follows:

360-400 points = A
320-359 points = B
280-319 points = C
240-279 points = D
239 points and below = F

Make-ups:	There are no make-ups for missed quizzes. If a student misses an exam, the student must contact the instructor immediately to arrange a make-up exam to be taken in the Testing Center within 48 hours of the original exam's start time. Failure to complete the make-up exam within this 48-hour period will result in a 10% penalty on the make-up exam grade.
Bonus Points:	30 bonus points will be given for each student who completes the online course evaluation for this course by the deadline stated on the attached calendar. To calculate the quiz average, 30 bonus points will be added to the student's total quiz points and then divided by twelve quizzes.
Cellphone Policy:	Cellphones must be turned off or muted during all class times. All cellphone use during class hours is strictly prohibited. Upon first violation of this policy, the student will receive a verbal warning. Upon second violation of this policy during the semester, the student will be required to leave class for the day and any missed quiz or exam that results from this violation will result in a zero grade (no make-ups allowed).
Bad Weather:	Upon inclement weather, please visit www.kowisstatecollege.edu or call (123) 456-7000 for the latest information on campus closings.

Course Calendar:

1/13: Chapter 1 & Appendix A / Quiz 1

1/20: Chapters 2 & 6 / Quiz 2

1/27: Chapters 7 & 8 / Quiz 3

2/03: Chapter 9 / Quiz 4

2/10: Chapter 10 / Quiz 5 / Review for Test 1

2/17: TEST 1

2/24: Chapters 11 & 12 / Quiz 6

3/03: Chapters 13 & 14 / Quiz 7

3/10: NO CLASS (Spring Break)

3/17: Chapters 15 & 16 / Quiz 8

3/24: Chapters 17 & 18 / Quiz 9

3/31: Chapter 19 / Quiz 10 / Review for Test 2

4/07: TEST 2

4/14: Chapters 36 & 37 / Quiz 11

4/21: Chapters 38 & 39 / Quiz 12

4/28: Review for Final Exam

Online Course Evaluation Is Due

5/05: FINAL EXAM (Cumulative)

This Course Calendar is ONLY A GUIDE. All dates, assigned chapters, exams, and quizzes are subject to change at the discretion of the Instructor. Any significant changes to this calendar will be announced in class, via email, or posted on the class webpage as soon as possible. It is each student's responsibility to come to all classes and keep up with any and all changes made to this calendar.

PRO TIP 2: Structure the Syllabus around the Textbook

This sounds elementary, but course materials will be much easier to follow if they are structured around the assigned textbook. If your students are asked to purchase or rent an expensive textbook for the course, the least you can do is make them read it and test them on the important materials contained therein.

If you feel that a particular textbook does not adequately address the topics that you want to teach, you should find a better textbook and ask your dean for permission to use it for your class. If you can't find a better textbook available on the market, there are several textbook publishers that frequently seek out instructors to write their own textbook or will customize (e.g., remove unnecessary chapters) your existing textbook to meet your needs. Teaching from materials that are not contained in the assigned textbook may cause problems if your students cannot readily find the source for that information when they are preparing for their exam.

> **Spring 2002: He takes the information that is in the book and explains it in a different way to ensure that the entire class gets a good understanding of the material.**

> **Fall 2011: He thoroughly teaches the material in the book.**

PRO TIP 3: Be Firm but Fair

Once you give students proper notice of your classroom policies in the syllabus, you must enforce these policies consistently and fairly. Just like a good parent, it is imperative that you stick to house rules and apply them equally to every student in a given situation. Otherwise you may find your class filled with unruly students who do whatever they want regardless of classroom policies.

One way to reinforce house rules is to refer to your class syllabus whenever a student asks a question that is covered by the house rules. If you allow an exception that is not already stated in the syllabus, you can expect the same student or others to ask for additional exceptions. Every parent has experienced this phenomenon with their own children, and it is no less true when a teacher conducts a class.

PRO TIP 4: Be Flexible When Needed and Revise Future Syllabi

As long as there are no working crystal balls for sale on eBay or Amazon, there will always be unexpected events that play havoc with one's plans. When that happens during a class that you're teaching, you must take control of the situation and be flexible enough to correct course. Here are two times when I was faced with such a situation.

An ice storm once caused the college where I teach to cancel all classes for a short time. I had suddenly lost a whole week of class and had to figure out how to teach all of the scheduled topics over remaining weeks of the semester.

There were two alternative solutions to this problem. First, I could have skipped the assigned chapters for the week that was canceled and otherwise proceeded with the semester as originally scheduled. But this option would have caused my students to miss out on some topics that I normally teach. Alternatively, I could have continued to teach all of the scheduled topics in the normal order and then skipped the three-hour review session that I usually schedule for the week immediately prior to the final exam. It was a hard decision because this review session helps students solidify the information that was taught throughout the entire course (as I discussed in greater detail in Chapter 7). As much as I enjoy teaching that review session, I decided to skip it so that my students would have the benefit of learning all of the scheduled topics that we normally cover each semester. As a compromise, I still gave a brief (ten-minute) review session at the end of the last regular class.

In the second instance, my students were taking a major exam when one of them discovered that he was missing a page. This didn't seem like a major problem until I realized that the entire class was missing the same page, which just happened to contain several true/false questions comprising almost a quarter of the total exam points.

I calmly instructed my students to continue taking the exam and reassured them that the missing page would not hurt their test scores. When I later graded the exams, the class average was about six or seven points below the typical average for that exam. Like the situation above with the canceled classes, I was faced with an unexpected problem and had to be flexible in how to resolve it.

I had two choices: stick to the status quo as much as possible by grading only the questions that were included in the given test, or give the missing exam page to my students at a later time and thereby allow them the opportunity to boost their exam scores. Although sticking to the status quo would have been more convenient for me, my students wouldn't get the opportunity to learn from the questions on the missing exam page, and their exam grades would suffer compared to typical semesters where the full exam was given. Ultimately I decided to be flexible and allow my students the option of completing the missing page as a take-home assignment. For those students who chose this option, it allowed them the chance to boost their exam grades by taking the full 50-question exam that I intended to give them instead of the actual 38-question exam that they received. Unfortunately, this decision resulted in more work for me, but it was in the best interest of my students and the right thing to do.

If an issue arises during the semester that you didn't anticipate in your syllabus, you should revise your syllabus before the next semester to avoid confusion from future reoccurrences. Similarly, if you discover that your syllabus is too harsh or unclear on a particular point, you should revise it to correct those problems as well. Think of your syllabus as a living document that continually needs attention to grow and thrive. For example, very few of my students owned a cellphone when I started teaching in 2001. As cellphones became popular, and my students' phones started ringing at random times during class lectures, I inserted language into the course syllabus requiring all phones to be turned off or muted during class as well as clearly stated penalties for violating of this policy. Students want to learn, and they don't want to disrupt their classmates, so this simple change to the syllabus solved the problem completely.

PRO TIP 5: Remind Students of Semester Progress

Another useful tip is to frequently remind students of what topics have recently been covered and when they can expect to see those topics on the next daily quiz or test. For example, you can begin each class with a one-minute recap of the general topics covered in the previous class and state the number of classes remaining until the next major exam. This gentle reminder can be helpful to those students who need help with time management or otherwise tend to procrastinate when it comes to studying. It also provides an overall roadmap that allows students to see how the various materials fit together and helps them retain the course materials.

> **Fall 2006: I like how during each class, he will bring up material from the previous class to help the information stick.**

Checklist and Action Items

Select at least two Pro Tips from this chapter that you are willing to use when planning your next course. Under each tip that you select, write down specific details of how you plan to implement the tip. For example, perhaps you are interested in creating or revising the syllabus and course calendar for your next semester. Under the first tip below, write a brief description of a few key items that you want to include in your new syllabus/course calendar or add to your existing syllabus/course calendar.

Five Pro Tips for Planning a Successful Course:

1) Create a Concise Syllabus and Course Calendar

_____
_____
_____

2) Structure the Syllabus around the Textbook

_____
_____
_____

3) Be Firm but Fair

_____
_____
_____

4) Be Flexible When Needed and Revise Future Syllabi

_____
_____
_____

5) Remind Students of Semester Progress

_____
_____
_____

Conclusion

Mr. Kowis is the most interesting, intellectual teacher that I have ever met since I have been going to college. He encourages me to do better and have higher expectations in whatever I choose to do and not to mention that he makes law interesting! This college should have more teachers like him.

—Anonymous student evaluation from Spring 2005

The 44 tips in this book for teaching engaging college classes can be summarized into two simple actions:

1) Make an honest effort to entertain your students, such as by telling adult jokes, using the occasional curse word, using outrageous examples to illustrate concepts you're teaching, singing an occasional song, or doing anything else that makes your students smile or laugh from time to time.

2) Use the SL Method to fully engage your students and hone their critical thinking skills.

My wife often teases me by saying that I only like teaching college classes because it provides a captive audience for my corny jokes. That may be partially true—I do love making people smile and laugh. However, the three primary reasons are my genuine love of teaching, the personal satisfaction that I receive from helping students advance their formal education, and the fulfillment of my duty as a Christian to give back to others in the community.

My passion for teaching was first stirred up during my law school days when I took a part-time job as a teacher's assistant to earn a few extra bucks. In that role, I quickly realized how much I loved being in front of the classroom and helping students learn the same materials that I had learned in the prior school year. I found myself frequently laughing and smiling during the classes I taught. Ultimately, I came to the profound realization that if I was having such a good time in class, my students were probably enjoying it too.

Beginning with my very first semester of teaching college classes, I have been convinced that teaching is the most rewarding job I could do on this planet. I feel a great sense of accomplishment at the end of every semester because I was able to play some small part in the success of my students. Teaching is my way of touching other people's lives, and hopefully for the better!

Teaching is much more than just another job to me. It is a calling from God. It's no coincidence that my talents match up perfectly with that of a college instructor, and I sincerely believe that it is my duty as a Christian and a child of God to use my gifts and talents to help others.[12] In fact, I can think of no better way to help others than to teach. I make this statement with absolute confidence because I know how important a good education is to one's lot in life. In my own life and career, I have seen amazing opportunities open up thanks in great part to my formal education and training. Without this education, I would most likely still live in my small hometown and work in a manual labor job at a dangerous chemical plant nearby. That can be an honorable life for sure, but I knew deep down that it wasn't the life for me. I wanted to branch out and see the world. To take on a challenging and rewarding career. To raise my family in a place with greater opportunities for my children than I had growing up. Those goals would simply not be attainable without obtaining a formal education. By teaching college classes, I want nothing more than to help others get a good education and thereby reach their own professional and personal goals.

---

[12] According to 1 Peter 4:10, Christians are called to use their God-given talents to serve others. I try my best to fulfill this responsibility by using my God-given gifts of humor, public speaking, and legal knowledge to serve my Business Law students.

I'll leave you with one last thought. I think of my presentation of materials to a college class as similar to performing an entertaining and thought-provoking play in front of a live audience. The only difference is that I ask the audience to participate in the show along with me. The college classroom should not be a boring room where the instructor coldly recites the textbook from behind a raised podium and students quietly take notes in robotic fashion. Rather, the classroom should be viewed as a grand theatrical stage where the instructor and students alike share in the joy of learning and intellectual exploration. Peace out.

Spring 2005: This college could use more instructors with this kind of skill and energy.

Spring 2005: Mr. Kowis makes this subject both fun and interesting to learn. He brings in humor and excellent real-life examples to explain the subject matter. He has made what could have been a very long and boring subject come to life, and has included all of the students in the class during lectures and testing. Excellent teacher!

Fall 2006: Mr. Kowis teaches at a level that anyone can understand.

Fall 2007: Best teacher I have ever had, and I sincerely mean that. I don't know how to make Business Law fun, but he manages it. I have been thinking about going to law school since beginning this class.

Fall 2011: Mr. Kowis could whoop Chuck Norris. He is the CEO of Donkey Washers Inc. and is a closet Justin Bieber fan. Too bad the semester is going to be over. I look forward to Thursday nights in his class. Thought it was going to be a boring class because of the material. Man was I wrong. Best instructor ever.

Fall 2012: Mr. Kowis makes the learning experience fun by making funny comparisons to the material.

Fall 2013: I want to personally thank him for the approach he takes with ALL of his students. He takes the time to get to know each and every one of us by name. You don't often find that instructors do this, especially in a college setting. Continue to spread your contagious vibe and knowledge for years to come, sir! THANKS FOR A GREAT SEMESTER!!!

Spring 2015: Thanks mr Kwois, you learned me abunch about law and stuff [*sic*].

Spring 2016: This professor is pretty awesome! I was dreading this class, but he made it fun and a joy to go to every Tuesday. His shenanigans are funny and his remarks and comments are hilarious! I don't mind his style, and he keeps you awake! Especially when you have been at work for so many hours, sitting in traffic and then go to learn about business law (snore) until 9PM!!! Thanks Professor Kowis! Wish he taught other classes that I have to take!

Bibliography

Barkley, Elizabeth F. *Student Engagement Techniques: A Handbook for College Faculty*. San Francisco: Jossey-Bass, 2010. Print. [College instructors can benefit from reading this book because it offers a wide variety of practical tips and strategies to increase student engagement that can be utilized in almost every college classroom.]

Canfield, Jack, Mark Victor Hansen, and Amy Newmark. *Chicken Soup for the Soul: Teacher Tales: 101 Inspirational Stories from Great Teachers and Appreciative Students*. Cos Cob, CT: Chicken Soup for the Soul Pub., 2009. Print. [With 101 touching stories from award-winning teachers from all over the United States, college instructors will enjoy reading this fun book and be inspired to make a difference in the lives of their own college students.]

Carnegie, Dale. *How to Win Friends and Influence People*. New York: Simon and Schuster, 1981. Print. [This timeless book gives practical tips on how to become a more likeable person and how to influence others. College instructors can benefit from its useful tips that show how to win the respect and admiration of students and inspire them to work hard.]

Carter, Judy. *The Comedy Bible: From Stand-up to Sitcom: The Comedy Writer's Ultimate How-To Guide*. New York: Fireside, 2001. Print. [This helpful book is full of advice for how to develop your funny bone. Though it is intended for comedy writers and stand-up comics, it would also benefit college instructors who are humor-impaired.]

Copeland, Matt. *Socratic Circles: Fostering Critical and Creative Thinking in Middle and High School*. Portland, ME: Stenhouse, 2005. Print. [This book explains the background of the 2,400 year old Socratic teaching method and gives real-world examples of how it can be applied in primary and secondary classrooms.]

Ramsey, Dave. *Entreleadership: 20 Years of Practical Business Wisdom from the Trenches*. New York: Howard, 2011. Print. [This inspiring book explains Dave's secrets to becoming a successful leader and small business owner. His advice applies equally to show how college instructors can effectively lead and inspire their students.]

Rath, Tom, and Donald O. Clifton. *How Full Is Your Bucket?* New York: Gallup Press, 2004. Print. [This insightful book reveals many ways to increase positive interactions with others and reduce the negative ones. It offers several practical tips that college instructors can use to give praise and recognition to their students.]

West, Edie. *201 Icebreakers: Group Mixers, Warm-Ups, Energizers, and Playful Activities*. New York: McGraw-Hill, 1997. Print. [Though this book is intended for trainers, speakers, and group facilitators, it should also benefit college instructors who are looking for fun icebreaker games to start off their semester on the right foot.]

Thanks to Everyone Who Made This Book Possible

When I decided to write this book, I set an arbitrary one-year deadline to complete it. To make sure I didn't back down, I announced these plans to my friends, coworkers, and family on social media and in person, and I'm happy to say that most of them were supportive.

As the deadline passed, my manuscript was little more than a long article (only 57 pages). Obviously I had grossly underestimated how much time and effort it takes to write a book, especially while juggling two jobs and raising a family. Despite being embarrassed by my limited progress, I pressed on.

At the two-year mark, I found myself suffering from a serious case of writer's block and the anxiety that comes with it. At this point, I had strung together 80 pages and a working title that I liked. However, I had run out of ideas to write about and desperately needed a muse to intervene. I sought help from freelance editor and book doctor, Mr. Geoff Smith. With his insightful guidance and developmental edits, I found my stride again.

As year three passed, the manuscript reached 113 pages and again I found myself struggling to come up with additional material to finish the book. For a second time, I sought the help of my amazing editor, Mr. Smith. He resurrected my dream from the bottom of the grave by providing fresh insights that I needed to continue writing.

Almost four years after I started, I finally wrapped up the rough draft and sought feedback from my wonderful friends, fellow professors, and former professors, including Dr. Robert Rich, Dr. Timothy Clipson, Dr. Sandy Farmer, and Mr. Richard Hunting. Mr. Smith provided the final "spit and polish" by working his copyediting magic and providing sage advice.

In summary, this book would not have been possible without the extraordinary help and support of many folks, including those mentioned above and my dear friends, coworkers and family. I would especially like to thank my beautiful wife, Jessica, and our two fun-loving children, Lauren and Cash, for putting up with me during this long and arduous process as well as allowing me the opportunity to teach night classes once a week at the local college.

About the Author

By day, Mike Kowis, Esq., is a mild-mannered tax attorney for a Fortune 500 company in Texas. By night, he swaps a three-piece suit for a pair of tights and a shiny red cape and then begins his duties as a modern-day SUPERHERO (aka Adjunct Faculty Member) for one of the largest community colleges in the Lone Star State. His superpower is ENGAGING COLLEGE STUDENTS in Business Law and Corporate Tax classes. He has spent the past 15 years fearlessly fighting for truth, justice, and the American way! Well, not really. But he has spent that time trying to fully engage his college students in night classes, which is just as hard.

In this, his debut book, Mike Kowis, Esq., shares the secrets to his success in the college classroom. If you have any questions or comments about this book or would like Mr. Kowis to speak at an event, please email him at mike@engagingcollegestudents.com, find his author page on Facebook (Mike Kowis, Esq.), or visit his website at www.engagingcollegestudents.com.

Dedication

To my loving parents, Pat and Tommie, who taught me that anything is possible with hard work and determination.

Thank you for being great role models!